EXPLORE
NEW MEXICO

INSIDER'S GUIDE: Getaways in the Land of Enchantment

Produced and designed by Richard C. Sandoval

Book edition edited by Ree Sheck
Typesetting by Linda J. Vigil
Map illustrations by Karen Gillis Taylor

Published by

NEW MEXICO MAGAZINE

First paperback edition 1989
by New Mexico Magazine

Copyright © 1989 by New Mexico Magazine

Published by New Mexico Magazine

ISBN: 0-937206-08-3

New Mexico Magazine
1100 St. Francis Drive
Santa Fe, New Mexico 87503

Library of Congress Catalog
Card Number 88-090889

Cover—*El Santuario de Chimayó.*
Photograph by Mark Nohl.

CONTENTS

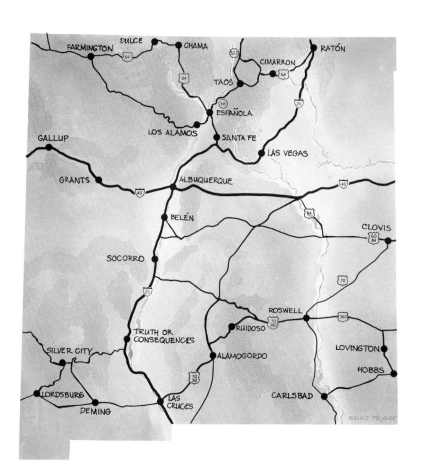

INTRODUCTION

Whether you are planning your first visit to New Mexico or count the Land of Enchantment as your home, this guide is designed to give you a taste of the trails waiting for you to explore. Visits to 27 hub cities lead you over much of the state.

In rural Spanish villages, Indian pueblos, ghost towns, mining towns, towns flavored with the Old West and the New West, and the state's larger cities, you can experience the history and the now. You can visit centers of art, old hotels snatched back from abandon and decay, space-age laboratories, museums large and small. The guide outlines special events to plan your trip around and suggests nearby attractions you may want to visit.

Once outside the towns and cities, trails lead to world-famous caverns, mysterious Indian ruins, spellbinding wildlife sanctuaries and a wealth of national and state parks and monuments. From the high mountains to the plains to desert lands, the guide suggests things to do and see.

Writers from around the state were commissioned by the editors of *New Mexico Magazine* to explore particular places and share their discoveries. The articles they wrote, along with those by Marc Sani, former publisher, and editors Emily Drabanski and Jon Bowman, appeared in the magazine over a two-year period and are presented here with photographs to give you a visual sense of each area's beauty.

A map for each area indicates major roads and surrounding towns. In an easy-to-use summary of practical information about each destination are data on population, climate—including high and low temperatures for summer and winter—and elevation, as well as special events and nearby attractions.

Buen viaje—good traveling—as you explore New Mexico, the Land of Enchantment.

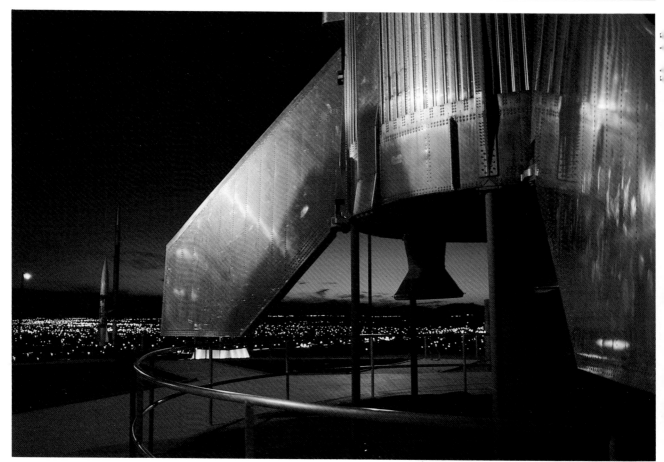

Alamogordo at night, seen from the base of a rocket outside the International Space Hall of Fame. The city is in the heart of the Tularosa Basin, a scenic setting for an interesting weekend.

Alamogordo

by Marc Sani

What began in 1898 as the key link for the El Paso and Northeastern Railroad has grown into the Southwestern city of Alamogordo—a unique community nestled in the historic Tularosa Basin. Flanked on the east by the towering Sacramento Mountains and on the west by a shimmering white sand desert, Alamogordo boasts many tourist attractions.

A weekend tour should include a visit to the International Space Hall of Fame and the Clyde W. Tombaugh Space Theater, both part of New Mexico's highly acclaimed Space Center, as well as the Alameda Park Zoo and the Otero County Historical Museum.

North of Alamogordo on US 54, visit the old Spanish towns of La Luz and Tularosa, Three Rivers Petroglyph National Recreation Site and the Valley of Fires State Park. South and east of the city, side trips to the Sunspot Solar Observatory, Oliver Lee Memorial State Park and spectacular White Sands National Monument will complete your visit to this historic area of New Mexico.

Alamogordo—Spanish for "fat cottonwood"—sits astride US 54/70, which as US 70 forks southwest to Las Cruces past White Sands National Monument and as US 54 goes south to El Paso and Ciudad Juárez.

The city began as a railroad mecca and grew quickly with the lumber industry, supplying all the railroad

White Sands National Monument varies from mysterious to brilliant, depending on the light.

Alamogordo's economy is based on tourism and government-related industries that service nearby Holloman Air Force Base and White Sands Missile Range. From Alamogordo, stunning recreational attractions can be found in any direction—from White Sands National Monument to alpine mountain resorts. Alamogordo is approximately 70 miles from Las Cruces and the border cities of El Paso, Texas, and Juárez, Mexico.

POPULATION: Approximately 28,000.

ELEVATION: 4,350 feet above sea level.

TERRAIN: Semidesert with alpine mountains to the East.

CLIMATE: Winters are mild with average temperatures of 57 degrees during the day and 28 at night. Warm summers average 95 degrees during the day with a cool nighttime average of 65.

PRECIPITATION: Annual average is 10.6 inches.

NEARBY ATTRACTIONS: White Sands National Monument, Lincoln National Forest, Oliver Lee Memorial State Park, Three Rivers Petroglyph Site, Sacramento Peak Solar Observatory, International Space Hall of Fame, Tombaugh Space Theater and the Tularosa Basin Historical Society Museum.

ties used in New Mexico. Alamogordo was propelled into the 20th century on July 16, 1945, at 5:30 am with the explosion of the first atomic bomb in the desert northwest of the city, and in March 1982, the space shuttle Columbia landed at nearby White Sands Space Harbor. Today, Alamogordo's history is linked to the stars through its Space Center, a division of the state's Office of Cultural Affairs. Situated on the northeastern edge of the city, space-age Saturn rockets loom in front of the center. Star of the complex is the International Space Hall of Fame, a brilliant "golden cube" honoring the men and women who have dedicated their lives to space research. More than 175,000 visi-

tors a year stop to look at the moon rock exhibits, space capsules and other displays that tell the stories of scientists, explorers and space pioneers who led man further than he once deemed possible. The exhibit Blazing New Trails focuses on the space programs of the 1960s—the Gemini, Mercury, Apollo and Russian space missions. The At Home and at Work in Space exhibit displays projects from the 1970s, including a miniature walk-through space station and exhibits of America's Space Shuttle program.

One of the Space Center's most popular attractions is the Clyde W. Tombaugh Space Theater, a planetarium and OMNIMAX® motion picture system, the only one of its kind within a 500-mile radius. The Tombaugh theater, named after the discoverer of Pluto, is a technological marvel featuring a four-story-wide, wrap-around screen and a six-channel audio system. In addition to the OMNIMAX® full-length feature films, the theater offers original planetarium programs and laser light shows and concerts.

Near the hall is Astronaut Memorial Garden, honoring the seven astronauts killed in the explosion of the space shuttle Challenger, and the John P. Stapp Air and Space Park, where visitors can see Sonic Wind One, the rocket sled ridden by Stapp in 1954.

Returning to the center of Alamogordo, you will find the Otero County Historical Museum, the Chamber of Commerce and the two-mile-long Alameda Park Zoo adjacent to this city center. The zoo is the oldest in the Southwest, established in 1898. It boasts more than 200 animals, plus a new waterfowl exhibit, and is part of a major effort to breed the rare Mexican gray wolf. Visitors will find picnic tables, barbecue pits, restrooms and other facilities at this seven-acre park.

However, it is the 230 square miles of drifting white gypsum sands 14 miles southwest of Ala-

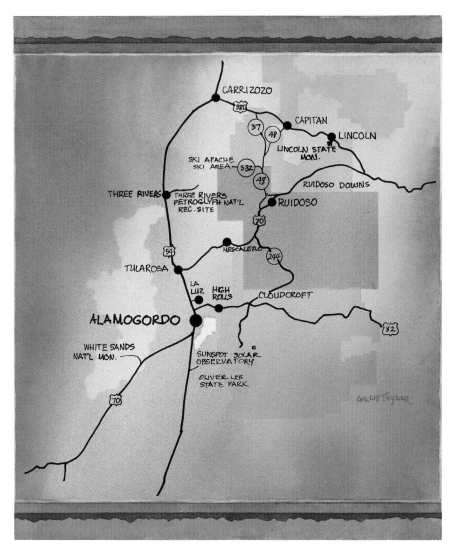

mogordo that attract national and international attention. Only 20 minutes from downtown Alamogordo, visitors will find dunes rising 50 feet in height. White lizards burrow in and out of the fine white gypsum grains, black beetles leave tiny footprints in the soft sand and a few hardy yucca plants and cottonwoods take root, defying the rythmic sweep of the shifting sand.

The world's largest expanse of gypsum hosts extraordinary plant species and unusual animal life. Rangers at White Sands, part of the National Park system, provide a variety of guided walks and evening talks to explain this unique ecosystem. A 16-mile

scenic drive dubbed "The Heart of the Dunes" is a traveler's guidepost to the wide-ranging shift in the life of the sands. At drive's end, you will find sheltered picnic tables and fireplaces, an ideal chance to stop and relax. For those who wish to spend a night under the stars in the heart of this desert environment, a primitive backcountry campsite is maintained by the park service. The monument is open every day of the year except for Christmas Day.

Continuing the tour, return to Alamogordo and then drive 15 miles south on US 54 to Oliver Lee Memorial State Park, an area steeped in Western lore. Here the Mescalero Apaches fought the United States

Cavalry, an eccentric Frenchman settled in Dog Canyon in the 1880s to raise grapes and cattle—he was later killed in a water rights dispute— and rancher Oliver Lee established his headquarters a quarter-mile south of Frenchy's Cabin. There are hiking trails, a visitor center, a museum, picnic facilities and an overnight RV facility.

Another side trip from Alamogordo begins north of town on US 82. The road east leads into the Sacramento Mountains, where visitors can enjoy the alpine village of Cloudcroft. A unique stop for astronomy buffs is the Sacramento Peak Observatory in Sunspot, south of Cloudcroft. Turn off on NM 130 and look for NM 6563 two miles from the turnoff. Follow it to the observatory. Located at an elevation of 9,200 feet, the observatory serves as a national center for scientists who study the sun. Equipment at the site includes some of the world's most sophisticated solar observation telescopes. A 350-foot-long Vacuum Tower Telescope that weighs 250 tons lets scientists observe solar details with unprecedented accuracy. A self-guided tour takes visitors to the telescope and Big Dome and provides a dramatic scenic view over the Tularosa Basin.

As you return from the observatory to Alamogordo, you will drop more than 4,300 feet in elevation during the descent along US 82. Visitors pass through vegetation zones that range from conditions unique to the Hudson Bay region of Canada to Mexico's Sonora Desert. This scenic drive also winds through the village of Mountain Park, where Bill Mauldin, the creator of World War II's cartoon heroes Willie and Joe, lived as a boy.

North of Alamogordo off US 54 is the old Spanish village of La Luz. Founded in the early 1700s, it is the oldest living settlement in the Tularosa Basin. In La Luz, an art center, visitors will find the church of Our Lady of Light, named after a small chapel built by two Franciscan friars in 1719. Farther north is the village of Tularosa, settled in the mid-1800s. At both villages, adobe buildings abound. A network of *acequias* (ditches) continue to irrigate crops, and folk artists carry on the tradition of Spanish colonial arts. Tularosa shares its name with the basin, a 200-mile-long lowland between the Sacramento Mountains to the east and the San Andrés Mountains farther to the west.

Seventeen miles north of Tularosa lies Three Rivers, a crossroads that began as a train station for wealthy ranchers. A century ago Patrick Coghlan, King of the Tularosa, and Susan McSween Barber, Cattle Queen of New Mexico, lived in this magic valley. They left a legacy of legends that includes murders, suicides, unexplained corpses, ghostly tales and bankrupt millionaires. And after Senator Albert B. Fall bought them out, he added a dollop of infamy to New Mexico history for his alleged role in the Teapot Dome Scandal.

Continuing north to Three Rivers, take a 16-mile side trip to Three Rivers Petroglyph National Recreation Site. A thousand years ago Mogollón Indians etched designs into the rocks. Today, no one knows the meaning of the Expressionist-like images these ancient Indians left, or why they abandoned the area about A.D. 1300. The dramatic scenery and sweeping views give these rock-strewn rises the status of sacred ground. Visitors can view the ancient rock art by walking a mile-long trail that passes among more than 500 petroglyphs.

Returning to US 54 north, visitors can catch glimpses to the left of the southern *malpais,* or badlands. About 2,000 years ago, a cubic mile of molten lava flowed out of a small peak at the north end of the Tularosa Basin and covered 127 square miles of land with rivers of basalt. As it cooled, the lava hardened into strange shapes that resemble everything from prehistoric monsters to mud pies. Today, at the Valley of Fires State Park just west of Carrizozo on US 380, a well-marked nature trail leads visitors through a small section of the *malpais.* A network of ancient Indian trails once crossed the *malpais,* but the sharp rock turns footwear to ribbons, and visitors are advised to stay on the nature trail.

As you return to Alamogordo along US 54, relax and enjoy the highlights of your visit to the unique lowlands of the Tularosa Basin and the highlands of the ancient Sacramento Mountains.

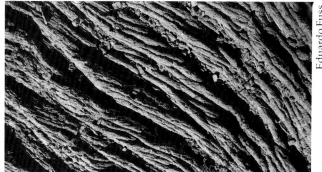

A detail of the Malpais' black volcanic rock offers a striking contrast to White Sands.

A walkway overpass on Third Street makes it easier for pedestrians to get around in downtown Albuquerque. The building at the left is City Hall.

Albuquerque

by Rusty Brown

The rugged face of the Sandía Mountains and the gentler slopes of the Manzanos . . . vistas of mesas that stretch to the row of spent volcanoes on the western horizon . . . a green belt of cottonwoods along the Río Grande.

These are the soul-food parameters of the sundrenched city of Albuquerque.

Legend has it that the city began with a fib and almost ended with a flood.

In 1706 Francisco Cuervo y Valdés, a New Mexico provincial governor, decided to make a name for himself by founding a town. He exaggerated when he wrote the Duke of Alburquerque, viceroy of New Spain, claiming a thriving settlement with a spacious

church and more than 30 families, the minimum required to be chartered as a villa under Spanish colonial law.

Actually there were only about 15 families, but to win approval and gain favor, Cuervo y Valdés told the viceroy the town was to be named for him. (And so it was, although the first *r* was dropped in the early 1800s.)

Despite the deception, Albuquerque did begin to attract more settlers and the town grew as a welcomed stopover for the caravans of soldiers, explorers, pioneers and traders traveling the Camino Real, the trail from Santa Fe to Mexico.

In 1846, the American flag was raised on the plaza and the territory annexed by the United States government. Albuquerque became a military garrison and an expanding cattle and wool center, yet its future was seriously threatened by periodic flooding. The one that almost drowned the town came in 1884. The cresting Río Grande washed away a bridge and temporarily knocked out the new railroad.

Yet the frontier settlement, now called Old Town, managed to survive the catastrophies of floods, politics and economic reverses. Much of the original character remains today in this preserved and restored community two miles west of "new" downtown Albuquerque.

The tree-shaded plaza is still in the same spot, now enhanced with a graceful white gazebo and wrought-iron benches for resting and people-watching. Original sections of San Felipe de Neri Church and its rectory that both face the plaza are nearly 200 years old.

Many of the surrounding homes, built a century or more ago in Territorial and Queen Anne styles, have been converted into art galleries, gift shops and restaurants with Southwest specialties. Narrow side streets and hidden patios, gardens and Spanish balconies further intrigue the visitor.

Be sure to browse the alleyway south of the Armijo house (La Placita restaurant) at the southeast corner of the plaza. The traditional placita, or compound, is where early settlers lived side by side for protection. A well in the center provided water in case of siege and the wide entryway to the placita allowed two-wheeled carts and livestock to pass through.

The compound now features curio shops, and Indians sell their turquoise and silver jewelry on the sidewalk under a nearby portico.

As a reminder of earlier days, Old West gunfights are staged year-round on Sunday afternoons along North Romero Street. At fiesta times, mariachi bands stroll the streets and dancing señoritas twirl their colorful, ruffled skirts to the swift rhythms of Spanish music.

Old Town becomes a fairyland on Christmas Eve when thousands of *farolitos* (small candles in paper bags, also known in Albuquerque as *luminarias*) line the streets and rooftops.

Adjacent to Old Town, on Mountain Road, are the city's two principal museums.

Life-size figures of two Spanish *conquistadores* in chain mail and armor—one of them on horseback—form a tableau at the Albuquerque Museum, dramatizing a turning point in New Mexico's history. That was the arrival of Francisco Vásquez de Coronado and his soldiers on a quest for gold in 1540. It marked the beginning of the Spanish colonization that forever changed the lives of the Tiwa Indians living in pueblos along the Río Grande.

The scene is the centerpiece of a permanent exhibit titled Four Centuries: A History of Albuquerque. Note early Spanish maps of the new-found wilderness; the Spanish treasure chests, once filled with pearls and coins; the paintings of saints, called *retablos*, that early settlers kept in their homes.

The museum displays paintings of major New Mexico artists including Carl Redin, Georgia O'Keeffe, Peter Hurd and Wilson Hurley and has constantly changing exhibits of art masterpieces and rare collections from around the world.

From May through October, museum docents conduct tours of Old Town, starting at the museum at 11:00 am, Wednesday through Friday, and at 1:00 pm weekends. Walking the streets of the oldest settled neighborhood in Albuquerque, visitors learn about the history and architecture.

The New Mexico Museum of Natural History is Albuquerque's newest—and oldest—attraction. The striking, sand-colored building with slanted roofs is what's new—it opened in January 1986. What's old is what's inside—an imaginative and chronologically organized paleontological history of the state beginning four-and-a-half billion years ago.

Want to experience a volcano? Just walk in and "feel" the river of red-hot lava swirling beneath the glass floor. Or clamber through a cool Ice Age cave ribbed with authentic-looking stalactites and stalagmites.

An 85-foot-long flowing replica of the Río Grande traces its journey from its source in Colorado all the way to Texas.

A full-sized model of Quetzalcoatlus looms over the central atrium. The 100-million-year-old New Mexico native had a 38-foot wingspan, making it the largest reptile that ever flew. There's also the skeleton of a 10-ton mammoth unearthed in Tucumcari in 1929.

If the museum has an aura of an amusement park, it is no accident. Some exhibits were inspired by, or actually built by, artists who helped create Disneyland.

You can go wild in Albuquerque at Río Grande Zoological Park, one of the finest small zoos in the country.

Meet Moonshadow, the snow leopard, lying regally beside a waterfall, or watch the cheetahs luxuriate in their shady habitat of tall grasses under the cottonwood trees. Catch Jamie, the gorilla, thumping on his

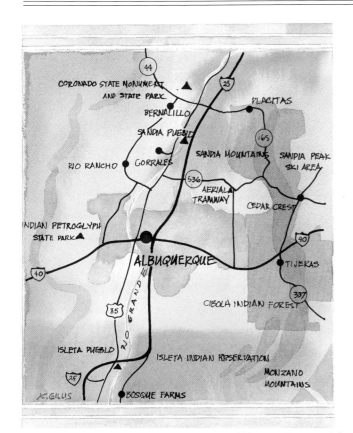

Top right—Gunfighters gather for a shootout in Old Town. **Bottom, right**—Giraffes and other animals entertain visitors at the Río Grande Zoological Park.

chest, and listen for the California sea lions barking for mackerel from their cool pool. It's all at the zoo, the city's proud gem on 10th Street, off Central.

The entrance sets the mood. Lush vegetation and a half-dozen waterfalls lead to the 60 sprawling acres where more than 1,000 animals live.

Just ahead, rose-pink flamingos stalk a quiet pond encircled with golden bamboo and the low-hanging branches of a corkscrew willow.

Don't miss the building to the left that houses a steamy rain forest. Enter under the waterfall and watch for flashes of brilliance as colorful tropical birds fly in and out of the dense foliage, calling to each other above your head.

Youngsters may pet a lamb or ride a camel and learn that its humps store fat, not water. And who cannot grin looking over Prairie Dog Town where those cute-faced residents pop in and out of their holes and chase around like windup toys?

Experience New Mexico's Native American heritage at the Indian Pueblo Cultural Center, owned and operated by New Mexico's 19 pueblos and located near the 12th Street exit off I-40.

Designed in the semicircular manner of the prehistoric Pueblo Bonito, a treasured ruin at Chaco Canyon, the building includes an Indian crafts bazaar and a museum commemorating centuries of Pueblo survival. Primitive tools made of stone, antlers, bone and wood are exhibited along with faded pottery shards. Contemporary crafts from each of today's pueblos also are displayed: crocheted dance leggings, moccasins, drums, beaded necklaces and painted bowls.

Indian dances—to the stirring accompaniment of beating drums—are staged summer weekends through mid-October. Bells, shells, feathers and fox skins decorate the costumes of the male dancers; women wear the traditional one-shouldered *manta* with handwoven sash. Both are bejeweled in ceremonial turquoise and silver.

A lunchroom offers a menu of Indian favorites including blue-corn enchiladas, posole and Indian bread pudding.

Just a few miles from the hustle of commerce and rush-hour traffic downtown lies the amazing bosque—acres of forest, open sand flats and meadows alongside the Río Grande. Here the beavers colonize at the river's oxbow, the crescent-shaped bend. Stands of 100-year-old cottonwood, Russian olive and feathery tamarisk thrive in the turf of silt and sand—along with Gambel quail, roadrunners, owls and coyotes. In fall and spring, the river marks the flyway for migrating Canada geese, sandhill cranes and whoopers.

The migrating birds often rest in the bosque on a three-acre pond beside the Río Grande Nature Center, a low dwelling built unobtrusively into the terrain at the river end of Candelaria Boulevard. One glass-walled room overlooks the pond and the activity of ducks, geese, bullfrogs, Western painted turtles and an occasional muskrat. Exhibits explain the ecology of the area, the anatomy of a leaf and how the bosque moderates temperature.

Two miles of trails surround the center and every Sunday at 1:00 pm, naturalists lead walks through the bosque to the river. Free admission.

Albuquerque is home of the University of New Mexico founded in 1889. UNM also is an architectural showpiece and many Albuquerqueans consider it a must-see for out-of-town visitors.

A suggested mini-tour begins at the parking lot beside the Maxwell Museum of Anthropology (free admission), where there's an excellent permanent exhibit chronicling the history of the Southwest.

Follow campus walks past the cluster of older buildings designed in the best of the Spanish-Pueblo tradition by famed architect John Gaw Meem. The alumni memorial chapel stands out as a charming prototype of Pueblo mission churches with its traditional carved-wood front balcony and twin bell towers. Continue over the grassy knoll and across the duck pond to stately Zimmerman Library, with tiered stories of adobe, colonnaded portals and flagstone patio. Enter through the modern glass doors of the new wing and turn left to the smaller, original section built in 1937.

The ceiling in the old lobby is a replica of the one at Ranchos de Taos church. Indian artisans crafted the intricate carved designs on the huge corbels and vigas. Note the handsomely carved doors, reference room desk and bookcases. Renowned artist Kenneth Adams painted the lobby murals, depicting the distinctive contributions of each of our three cultures: Indian, Spanish and Anglo.

A major artery, Grand Avenue, quickly connects UNM with downtown. The view from the Grand Avenue overpass is striking: modern office buildings and the Albuquerque Convention Center in desert colors, interspersed with sleek walls of glass.

There's the spacious Civic Plaza to see, between Tijeras and Marquette Streets, distinguished by a handsome fountain and edged with trees, blooming gardens and modern municipal buildings. Across the plaza is the two-block-long pedestrian parkway called Crossroads, where office workers spend lunch hours meeting, eating and shopping.

Be sure to swing by the ornate New Mexico Title Building (formerly Occidental Life) on Gold Avenue, designed in 1917 by Henry Charles Trost to resemble the Doge's Palace in Venice. Glazed white terra cotta tile faces the recently renovated landmark, giving it the look of marble.

Two more treasures are the old Federal Courthouse at Fourth and Gold, with its two-story arched entranceway and red-tiled roof, and the 1927 movie house in Pueblo Deco style, the garish KiMo Theatre at Central and Fifth.

Not to be missed: the restored hotel lobby of the Territorial-style La Posada de Albuquerque at Second and Copper, formerly the old Albuquerque Hilton. Note the massive carved vigas, lobby fountain, encircling balcony and fixtures of etched glass and tin. Be sure to tell visitors that this is where the flamboyant '30s mayor Clyde Tingley liked to hold court and where Conrad Hilton honeymooned with actress Zsa Zsa Gabor.

Albuquerque is a corridor through time—through billions of years of roiling seas, volcanic eruptions and the arrival and extinction of the dinosaur.

It also is a corridor through 10,000 years of human habitation. Paleo-Indian hunters stalked mammoths and bison along the muddy "great river." Unearthed pit houses (semisubterranean lodges) and mountain caves have yielded remnants of these prehistoric residents including stone tools, flint chips and fire pits. In time, the Anasazi evolved to become the Tiwa Indians who, by 1300, had built pueblos up and down the Río Grande.

The most apparent clues to the ancient ones are found in the 10,000 petroglyphs scattered around the city's West Mesa. Visitors can see this remarkable rock

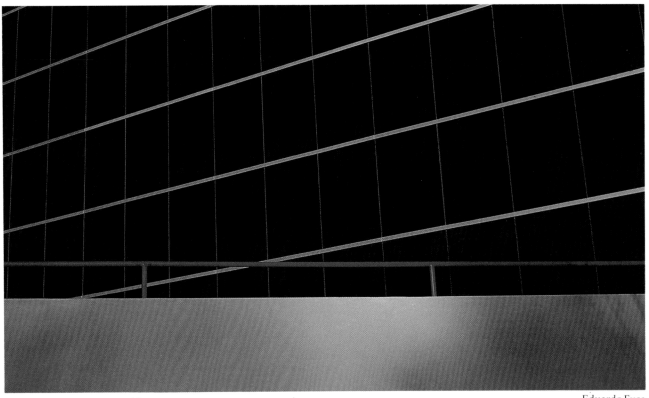

Detail of a building in uptown Albuquerque.

Eduardo Fuss

art at Petroglyph State Park at Atrisco Road, northwest of the Coors Road exit from I-40.

The drawings are engraved into the stones of a lava flow from a volcanic eruption a million years ago. Experts say the artwork dates from A.D. 1100 to 1600 and theorize that the ancestors of today's Pueblo Indians hunted in the area, taking shelter at night on the hill of lava rocks and boulders. To pass the time, they used stone chisels to peck out pictures of animals, birds and insects, symbols for sun and clouds, handprints and simple drawings of themselves and their gods.

The asphalt trail of this open-air gallery ascends gradually to the top of the lava pile, revealing drawings at every turn plus sweeping views of the city, the Sandías and Manzano Mountains.

If scratched rocks are not your thing, how about smashed atoms? The story of the nuclear era is covered at the National Atomic Museum at Kirtland Air Force Base. The top-secret Manhattan Project that was centered in New Mexico and culminated in the test of the atomic bomb is dramatically chronicled in the film *Ten Seconds That Shook the World*, produced by impresario David Wolper. Replicas of Little Boy and Fat Man, the atomic bombs dropped on Japan, are displayed, plus exhibits on types of energy such as solar, nuclear, fossil fuels, wind and tides. Call for movie times and tour arrangements.

Get a bird's-eye view of Albuquerque by riding to Sandía Peak (elevation: 10,378 feet) via the nation's longest aerial tramway. New tram cars, custom-made in Switzerland, feature more window space for experiencing the thrilling 2.7-mile ascent up the west side of the Sandías. The tram climbs over boulder-studded terrain and through steep-walled canyons before docking at the sky-top observation deck 18 minutes later.

Look up and you may see a golden eagle or a hang glider in flight. Look down and you may see bighorn sheep amid the junipers and piñons.

The geographic, financial and industrial center of the state, Albuquerque extends up and down the Río Grande Valley in the shadow of the Sandía and Manzano mountain ranges. The city is one of the fastest growing in the Southwest. Airline, rail and motor freight and two interstates provide direct connections to the Southwest, West Coast and Mexican markets.

POPULATION: Approximately 500,000 in the greater Albuquerque area.

ELEVATION: 5,311 feet above sea level.

TERRAIN: High semidesert plateau with mountains on the east and mesas on the west.

CLIMATE: Winters are mild and cool. Summer temperatures are hot in the day and cool in the evening. Typical January temperatures range from 46 degrees in the day to 28 degrees at night. In July, the average high is 91 degrees with nighttime temperatures at an average low of 66 degrees.

PRECIPITATION: Annual average is 8.1 inches.

SPECIAL EVENTS: Annual Río Grande Valley Bicycle Tour, Río Grande Raft Race, Charley Pride Senior Golf Classic, Celebration of the Arts, Indian Pueblo Cultural Center Arts & Crafts Fair, Santo Domingo Feast Day, Fiesta Artística, New Mexico State Fair, Albuquerque International Balloon Fiesta, Southwest Arts & Crafts Festival and Christmas Eve Luminaria Tour.

The observation deck offers spectacular top-of-the-world views across 100 miles of mesas, volcanoes and mountains, including majestic Mount Taylor, sacred to the Navajos. Five thousand feet below, the Río Grande glistens and I-40 stretches beyond the horizon like a ribbon to the end of the earth.

Sandía Peak also is the terminus of the ski trail chairlifts approaching from the eastern slope of the mountain. A wintertime bonus is watching skiers in colorful garb maneuver off the chairlifts and onto the ski trails.

There's a restaurant at the summit, High Finance, serving lunch and dinner in a glass-walled dining room.

In good weather you can hike the 1½ miles from Sandía Peak to Sandía Crest through the Cíbola National Forest. En route (allow 45 minutes) take Crest Trail #130 that passes partly through woods and, at one point, crosses a vast meadow with marvelous views all the way to Santa Fe and the Sangre de Cristo Mountains. At the Crest (10,610 feet), there's a lookout and gift and snack shop. To return, take the path that drops to La Luz Trail (it's well-marked) and follow La Luz back to the tram.

Another way to get to the top is to drive up the other side of the mountain. Take I-40 through Tijeras Canyon, the same route followed by Indian traders and the forty-niners. Exit at NM 14 and drive through Cedar Crest and the foothills. Watch for signs pointing to Sandía ski trails and NM 536. Turn left on NM 536, a winding, scenic drive to Sandía Crest.

Back in the city, it's not exactly San Francisco's trolley ride. There are no steep hills and it runs on tires, not cables. But Albuquerque's Molly Trolleys look like turn-of-the-century cable cars and offer a convenient and quaint way to get to some of the city's principal tourist attractions, hotels and shopping centers.

The spiel of the trolley drivers is filled with anecdotes and tourist data that sometimes surprise even old-time Albuquerqueans. Pick up a schedule at hotels or Old Town.

While Albuquerque is steeped in tradition, today the city exudes a bustling, cosmopolitan flavor. It has become one of the high-technology centers of the Southwest and is a major crossroad for travel and industry. Restaurants range from home-owned New Mexican cafes to slick night spots. Albuquerque offers numerous cultural opportunities ranging from shows presented by the Albuquerque Gallery Association to performances by the New Mexico Symphony. Sports fans will find plenty of action at the Albuquerque Dukes'

Pat Berrett

baseball games and UNM Lobo football and basketball games.

The State Fairgrounds come alive with the flashing lights of the midway, the excitement of horse racing and rodeo action during the annual State Fair in September. Throughout the year numerous activities from art fairs to rock 'n' roll concerts take place at the fairgrounds. On weekends, bargain hunters can browse through one of the country's largest flea markets.

Special events fill the city's calendar. Some of the largest include: the spring Celebration of the Arts, Fiesta Artística in August, the Albuquerque International Balloon Fiesta in October and the Southwest Arts and Crafts Festival in November.

A weekend visitor will be hard-pressed to sample all the attractions mentioned here. In fact, if you get to everything—you're moving too fast!

Yet there are still other places of interest: Coronado State Monument, Corrales Village, North Valley estates, the Albuquerque Country Club area and Sandía, Santo Domingo and Isleta pueblos.

Eduardo Fuss

BALLOON FIESTA

Chasing the Clouds

Neither words nor wide-screen TV can capture the magnitude of the annual Albuquerque International Balloon Fiesta.

You have to be on the scene to feel the chill of the morning darkness and welcome the first rays of sun rising behind the Sandía Mountains to the east. You have to be there to enjoy the jostling of the crowd, the aroma of fresh-baked Indian bread and other pungent foods sold at booths rimming the launch site.

And, of course, be there to hear the whir of the big fans coaxing the balloons, lying shapeless on the ground, to rise like awakening giants for the ride to the sky. Camera bugs go bananas.

Most thrilling are the four ascensions on Saturday and Sunday mornings of the opening and closing weekends. For two hours after dawn, more than 500 balloons float over Albuquerque like an invasion of sugar plums—a palette of color across the sky.

Albuquerque, the Balloon Capital of the world, is especially suitable because of its high altitude, few obstructions and October winds that are steady but manageable.

Besides the mass ascensions on weekends, military sky divers and acrobatic airplanes present shows. During the week, the balloon pilots take part in spirited competitions, highlighted by the key-grab, when balloon jockeys vie to snatch new car keys hooked atop a 25-foot pole.

The fiesta is in October at a site between Paseo del Norte and Alameda Road, just west of I-25. Public parking is through the Alameda entrance.
—**Rusty Brown**

Prickly pear cactus near Carlsbad Caverns.

Photos by Mark Nohl

Carlsbad

by Colleen Rae

Run a plumb line down through Carlsbad's history, and water marks the course. Water shaped the area, leaving the limestone reefs the earth pushed up to form the highest peaks in the area. It brought the bison, and the Indians who hunted them. Water marked a trail for men driving cattle from Texas and attracted European immigrants to Carlsbad's fertile valleys in southeastern New Mexico. Water gave the town its name and created one of the biggest fairylands in the world—Carlsbad Caverns.

Imagine walking down, down, down into the throat of an unexplored cave, your path dimly lit, a beam of light playing off stalactites dripping like icicles and stalagmites thrusting up from the slick mud of the floor. That's what a cowboy named Jim White saw in 1901 when he discovered Carlsbad Cavern, the biggest cave in what became Carlsbad Caverns National Park.

Since the National Park Service took over, visitors to the cavern don't need lanterns. Well-placed lights bring soda straw forests and aragonite trees out of hiding. Paved paths skirt calcite lily pads.

Enter the cavern at the visitor center, 20 miles southwest of Carlsbad. There are two tour options: follow

White's trail through the cave mouth or take high-speed elevators from the visitor center and intercept the long trail in the underground lunchroom 750 feet below. The trip from the natural opening requires a bit of stamina—the trail is three miles long and the self-guided tour takes about three hours. The shorter self-guided tour takes about one and a half hours and loops a mile and a quarter around the Big Room.

Aptly named, the Big Room could hold 14 Astrodomes, and, at its highest point, the ceiling curves 256 feet above the floor. In October 1986, cave explorers climbed a rope to the dome and discovered a large unexplored area.

Even though the tours don't lead through uncharted realms, there's plenty to see. Wear warm clothes. The cavern is a constant 56 degrees. Since the cavern is a partially living cave still being etched out by groundwater seeping through the desert floor above, the paths can be slick. Comfortable walking shoes with nonskid soles should do the trick.

Carlsbad Caverns is open seven days a week, year-round, except for Christmas Day. Amenities include a nursery, kennel, bookstore, gift shop and restaurant.

For an experience closer to Jim White's, opt for New Cave. In groups of 25, rangers take visitors on a two-hour lantern tour. Since the cave is undeveloped, you must bring a flashlight and water. This is for people in good shape; the approximately half-mile walk takes you up a 500-foot incline to the entrance. Allow 30 to 45 minutes and wear sturdy shoes.

New Cave is open on weekends during the winter and daily from Memorial Day to Labor Day. The tour is not recommended for small children. Reservations are required.

From May through October, Carlsbad Cavern offers an unusual experience—bat flights. Nearly a million Mexican freetail bats spiral up from the cavern's mouth at night. Before the flights, park interpreters give information and humorous talks about the world's only flying mammal.

Each August, the Employees Association of Carlsbad Caverns hosts the Bat Flight Breakfast. It's a one-of-a-kind experience to sit enveloped in predawn black as the bats fall like dark shooting stars one after another into the cave's mouth.

Carlsbad Caverns National Park is the area's most famous attraction, but Living Desert State Park treats visitors to wonders as well. Those traveling south on US 285 will see signs for the park on the outskirts of Carlsbad. Turn right and follow Skyline Drive to the visitor center high in the Ocotillo Hills.

The park, open year-round, serves as a preserve for plants and animals indigenous to the Chihuahuan Desert. Lechuguilla, palm yucca and sotol grow in sand dunes, desert uplands and gypsum hills that stretch back from the paths. Javelina live in an enclosed arroyo, a black bear named Goldie soaks in her queen-size bathtub under a waterfall, endangered Mexican wolves roam marshes, ringtails and kangaroo rats explore the nocturnal exhibit.

On the trail to the prairie dog town and deer and elk enclosures, views of the basin stretching north, east and south are spectacular. Far below, Carlsbad hugs the winding Pecos River.

Mescalero Apaches spent a great deal of time in this area, hunting buffalo across the Pecos River and roasting mescal or agave. During the full moon in May, Living Desert State Park recreates the mescal roast in a special midden ring at the park, and visitors get to taste the product. Some say this roasted heart of the flowering century plant tastes like sweet potatoes with a smoky molasses flavor.

Returning to downtown Carlsbad, you'll find the city hall on Mermod Street. New Mexico's architect laureate, John Gaw Meem, designed this building and the gas company building a block and a half south on Halagueno.

Across the street from city hall you'll find the Carlsbad Public Library and the Carlsbad Museum and Art Center. Exhibits include the work of 10 artists from the original Taos artist colony and a large collection of artifacts and memorabilia donated by Merlee Hollebeke, a Delaware River-area rancher who traces her memories back to the late 1800s.

Take a tour of the downtown area. Carlsbad became part of the national Main Street program in 1986 and has turned its historic downtown into a showcase.

The brands around the west door of the Pueblo-style Eddy County Courthouse lay claim to Carlsbad's heritage. This is cowboy country.

During the late 1860s, cattlemen named Goodnight and Loving drove longhorn steers up the east side of the Pecos River to the present site of Carlsbad, where they forded the river and continued up the west bank to market. This area became known as Loving's Bend, after Loving was fatally wounded at the spot by Indians.

Legend has it that this site was christened Eddy in 1888 when Lillian Green, a daughter of one of the town's promoters, broke a bottle of champagne at this ford on the Pecos River.

The town was named Eddy for brothers John A. and Charles B. Eddy, local ranchers. The Eddy house can still be seen in La Huerta on Carlsbad's north side. Follow Canal Street north nearly to its end. From La Huerta Bridge, it's four miles to the plaque and old stone house on the left.

Ten years later, townspeople voted to rename the town Carlsbad—the result of a water analysis of the Pecos River that indicated the water's composition was the same as that in Carlsbad, Bohemia, now known as Karlovy Vary, Czechoslovakia.

It's a short distance from the Eddy house to Avalon Reservoir, one of the string of warm-water, man-made lakes along the Pecos. Others include Lake McMillan, 19 miles north of Carlsbad; Red Bluff Lake, 36 miles south, and Bataan Lake in town. They are good places to catch largemouth bass, catfish, crappie, white bass, walleye and stripers. From October to March, New Mexico Game and Fish stocks Bataan Lake with trout. Each December the city sponsors a fishing derby with local merchants providing cash and prizes for those catching tagged fish.

Hunters can enjoy the Carlsbad area as well. The mule deer season opens in November and lasts three weeks; dove season extends through September; quail, November through January. The best place for deer is the Guadalupe Mountains; quail, east of Carlsbad, and dove are everywhere.

Returning to Carlsbad, follow the scenic drive along the section of the Pecos River that's called Lake Carlsbad. Here you can picnic under giant pecan trees, boat, water-ski, play tennis or fish. Farthe

Top—*A view along the entrance road to Carlsbad Caverns National Park.* **Bottom**—*Speedboating on the Pecos River.*

down the river, there's a sandy beach area with high dives, water slides and a wading pool area. During summer, you can ride the George Washington, an authentic paddlewheel boat, or walk across the river on a pontoon bridge to Presidents' Park. This amusement park offers a 1903 carousel, the Roosevelt Raceway

Top—A mountain lion at Living Desert State Park, a zoological and botanical garden near Carlsbad.
Bottom—The Klansman, a stalagmite in New Cave at Carlsbad Caverns.

Lake Carlsbad serves as the site for River Fest in May. Events include water- and jet-skiing competitions, homemade raft and inner tube races, a speedboat show and a display of boats and recreational vehicles.

In June, the beach area makes a backdrop for the annual Art Affair, an arts and crafts show for Southwestern artists.

On July 4, the beach area really comes to life. During the day clowns entertain, volunteer fire departments vie for trophies and musicians entertain at the band shell. Evening brings a boat and flag parade, followed by what's billed as "the biggest and best fireworks display in southern New Mexico."

Other Carlsbad events include Western Week in mid-July and Alfalfafest in October. Both celebrate the ranching and farming traditions out of which Carlsbad grew.

During Western Week, townspeople dress in old-time Western garb and merchants decorate their stores with a Western motif. There are events such as a parade that includes refurbished covered wagons, a chile cook-off and a three-day American Junior Rodeo Association rodeo. Dances follow each night's rodeo.

Alfalfafest celebrates another Carlsbad lifeblood: one of the area's biggest cash crops—alfalfa. The day features a parade with "the world's biggest hayride," Farm Olympics, a fiddling contest and events such as a tug-of-war and an outhouse race.

For those tracing the trail of Carlsbad's history, there are several options. One is to drive north 12 miles on US 285 to NM 137, which heads out toward Sitting Bull Falls. The road winds through Rocky Arroyo where some of the area's first pioneers, the Jones' family, set-

Bumper Cars and the Abe Lincoln Train, a narrow-gauge steam train of 1880s vintage that takes passengers on a two-mile trip along the shores of Lake Carlsbad and the municipal golf course. Presidents' Park is open daily in summer and on holidays throughout the year.

tled. Some are buried in the cemetery there, including "Ma'am Jones of the Pecos," who doctored the early settlers and threw the best dances around. Billy the Kid was a friend of her son, John Jones, and spent time under her roof.

The road climbs from there toward Lincoln National Forest—through an area once densely populated with homesteaders—and on to a lone chimney stack, which is all that's left of Queen.

Down a dirt road lies a cemetery with some of the Queen family graves. Two Queen brothers supplied Queen's first owner, a man named Tulk, with water. In exchange, he named the town for them.

Along the side of Queens Highway near the turnoff to the cemetery, there's a large concrete monument with a propeller. It's worth the trip just to read about the flying "paperboy" who lost his life near that spot.

The Queens Highway continues through pine trees before it drops gradually into the valley ranched by the Hughes family for decades. After passing some of the Hughes' ranches, you can travel the back road to El Paso/Juárez or go on to Dog Canyon. The latter leads you to a National Park Service campground that has water, restrooms and overnight camping areas, including four flat spaces for recreational vehicles, but no RV hookups.

The road ends here on the New Mexico side of the Guadalupe Mountains. To see more of the grandeur of this range, you'll need to travel to the Texas-New Mexico border.

On the way back to Carlsbad, detour to Lincoln National Forest's Sitting Bull Falls, where you can picnic and watch a waterfall pour into pools at the base of an 80-foot-high cliff.

On the drive back to Carlsbad, take another short detour toward Artesia. Turn left on US 285 and drive north six miles to Seven Rivers, which was a watering

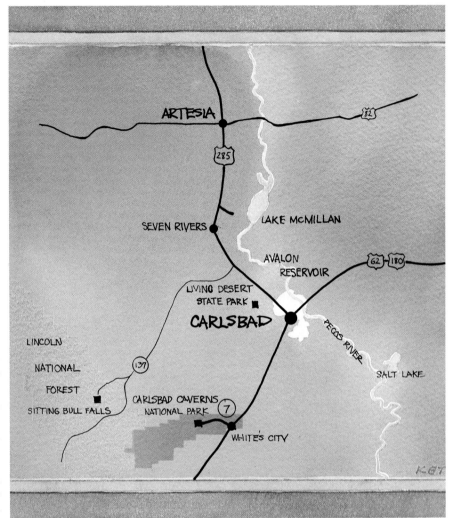

place on the Goodnight-Loving trail and site of the Jones family's trading post. Seven Rivers is the burial site for several of the area's early settlers. A roadside marker on US 285 tells some of the history.

Artesia, 36 miles north of Carlsbad, is a hub for oil and natural gas production. The Artesia City Museum houses history and art exhibits, while the Heritage Walkway mural in downtown Artesia traces the settlement and development of the region.

The history trail leads back through Carlsbad with a quick stop at Carlsbad's flume. Turn left on Callaway Drive a little south of the entrance to Living Desert State Park. When you get near the flume, take the right fork in the road and drive under the flume along the edge of the Pecos River. Make sure you have your camera because this aqueduct, with its four Roman arches reflecting on the surface of the river, inspires artists. Although the flume dates back to 1906, it's still a major part of the area's irrigation system.

Continue along the river a short distance, and you'll find what looks like a large concrete bathtub at the river's edge. This structure remains from Carlsbad's days as a spa.

Backtrack to US 285 and continue through town along Canal Street back out to the National Parks Highway to the Cavern City Air Terminal. Just past the airport on the left you will see signs for the Flying X Chuckwagon. From May through October you can get fare fit for a ranch hand's birthday: barbecue simmered in special sauce, baked potatoes, beans, chuck wagon biscuits, applesauce, ranch-style cake, cowboy coffee and lemonade. Following the meal, the Flying X Ranch Hands will entertain you with cowboy songs.

One and a half miles south of the airport on US 62/180 you'll find the Antique Auto Barn, a museum with more than 40 antique and classic autos and automotive items.

Continue along US 62/180 to White's City to see the Million Dollar Museum, with its collections of dolls and dollhouses, Old West memorabilia, 6,000-year-old mummified Indians and a two-headed snake. For live examples of rattlers, backtrack a short distance to White's City's Apache Canyon Trading Post.

The history trail leads to the visitor center at Carlsbad Caverns National Park, the starting place for the free, nine-and-a-half-mile Walnut Canyon Desert Drive. Each stop gives a different aspect of natural or man-made history—the cliffs of the Guadalupe Mountains with their geological saga, the effects of shade and sunshine, the remains of an ancient lagoon, miniature aboveground caverns, remnants of one of the first homesteads.

Continue south along US 62/180. On the right along County Road 418 in the direction of New Cave you'll find an oasis in the desert, Rattlesnake Springs. It's a bird-watcher's paradise, with more than 200 species. It's also a great place for a picnic.

Next stop: Guadalupe Mountains National Park just across the Texas border. This park once was covered by an inland arm of the sea. The warm, shallow waters near the edge created a reef, which fossilized as limestone. About 10 to 12 million years ago, this reef was pushed up and now forms the Guadalupe Mountains.

The park has 80 miles of trails for hiking, backpacking and horseback riding. You may see deer, black bear, elk and mountain lion within its borders. And it has a few interesting remnants from the Old West.

With its world-famous caverns nearby, Carlsbad is among the most popular tourist destinations in New Mexico. It's a sparkling, clean city, offering a moderate climate, warm hospitality and well-kept parks and picnic areas. Besides tourism, the Carlsbad economy hinges on agriculture, potash mining and the new Waste Isolation Pilot Project. Carlsbad is host to a growing retirement community. Nearby Artesia is a hub for oil and natural gas production.

POPULATION: Carlsbad, 28,400. Artesia, 13,960.

ELEVATION: Carlsbad, 3,110 feet above sea level. Artesia, 3,380 feet above sea level.

CLIMATE: July temperatures average in the mid 90s during the daytime, the mid 60s at night. In January, daytime temperatures average near 60, with temperatures dipping near 30 at night.

PRECIPITATION: 12.4 inches annually in Carlsbad, 15.2 inches in Artesia.

SPECIAL EVENTS: Western Days in Carlsbad in mid July, Bat Flight Breakfast at Carlsbad Caverns in August, Alfalfafest in Carlsbad in October and Arts in the Park fair in Artesia in October.

NEARBY ATTRACTIONS: Carlsbad Caverns National Park, Living Desert State Park, Sitting Bull Falls, Lake McMillan, Lincoln National Forest and Guadalupe Mountains National Park.

Brazos Cliffs south of Chama.

Chama & Dulce

by Marc Sani

T om Vigil eased his four-wheel-drive Bronco to a halt. This dirt road snaking through the heart of the Jicarilla Apache Reservation was slick with snow. As he slipped the gearbox into low-range, four-wheel drive, Vigil continued talking. "We want people to come visit our lands. We want them to stop and feel free to enjoy the solitude."

Solitude. You can't see it. You can't taste it. But in this ancient land, you can feel the timeless beauty. The Jicarillas take pride in welcoming the weekend visitor to their homeland, as do others who live in this rough-hewn, scenic central corridor of northern New Mexico.

Village names like Dulce, Chama, Monero, Brazos and Tierra Amarilla trip lightly off the tongue—their Spanish and Italian heritage cloaking close ties to the land. Tradition runs deep here where ranching, logging, sheepherding, hunting and fishing are the staples of economic life. No fancy boutiques, trendy restaurants or glitzy hotels have left their mark. A family can enjoy a weekend in the north without breaking the monthly budget.

But change is in the wind. Tourism plays an ever larger role in the economy of an area where lakes, mountains, meadows and heavy winter snowfall beckon the visitor as well as the entrepreneur. A few miles northeast of Tierra Amarilla, downhill ski runs have been cut through heavy forest growth anticipating a future ski bonanza. Vacation homes and undeveloped lots are for sale. But there is concern about the future. Some longtime residents oppose major development and worry about its impact on their families, culture and land.

Still, a visit here is a chance to slow down, enjoy a different pace of life. Cross-country ski or snowmobile in the winter, wander through summertime forests and meadows in search of mushrooms, climb above Cumbres Pass and marvel at its spectacular vistas, fish free-flowing streams, hunt deer and elk in season, water-ski or sail at El Vado or Heron lakes.

Several small airstrips dot the countryside, but you will need a car to take full advantage of this region. For the adventurous with four-wheel drive, dozens of dirt roads lead to sights seldom visited by tourists.

Travelers from the south can take US 84 from Española to Chama. US 64 from Farmington and Bloomfield leads east to Dulce and connects with US 84 to Chama. Visitors leaving from Taos take US 64 east over the spectacular Río Grande Gorge, through the pine-covered high country west of Tres Piedras and on to Tierra Amarilla, connecting with US 84 south of Chama. A word of caution—heavy snows have sometimes closed US 64 west of Tres Piedras. Check local driving conditions before taking this route. Those who leave from Durango, Colorado, can drive east on US 160 to Pagosa Springs, Colorado, turning south on US 84 to Dulce or Chama.

Dulce is the commercial center for the 2,500 Apaches who live on the Jicarilla Reservation— 750,000 acres of wild and rugged landscape dotted with lakes, ancient ruins and modern oil wells. "Apaches consider themselves mountain people," said Tom Vigil, who with his family, operates the Jicarilla Inn. Dirt roads crisscross this land that extends north to the Colorado border and south to NM 44 near Cuba. The reservation's boundaries extend east to Heron and El Vado lakes and, to the west, abut a portion of the Carson National Forest.

The Jicarillas have set aside 24,000 acres of rolling countryside flanked by gently rising hills for cross-country skiing, dogsledding and snowmobiling. The area is a few miles south of Dulce on the road to Stone Lake Lodge. In late winter it is often blanketed with up to three feet of snow. Visitors should first check in at tribal headquarters in Dulce or the Jicarilla Inn, the newest and most modern motel in the region. More than a half-dozen small lakes dot the reservation, some ideal for ice fishing. Again, check for directions, fees and advice.

The Anasazi—the Ancient Ones—once made their homes in this land that now belongs to the Jicarillas. Unrestored ruins, cliff dwellings and pictographs are scattered in remote areas on the reservation. Strong legs and good shoes are essential if you want to see them. Also visit the Jicarilla Apache Museum and Arts and Crafts Center in Dulce. One interpretation for the word Jicarilla is "little basket," and the Jicarillas are recognized for their intricate basket weaving. Visitors can purchase authentic baskets, beadwork, leatherwork and jewelry at the crafts shop.

The Jicarillas are proud of the record catches and trophy animals taken on their land. Spruce, Douglas fir, ponderosa pine, piñon, juniper and sagebrush cover the reservation. Mule deer, elk, bear, turkey and waterfowl are abundant, with steep mountains, remote canyons and broad valleys creating an ideal wild game habitat. Ponds and lakes provide a haven for waterfowl, but duck hunters must use steel shot. The Jicarillas strictly control outside hunting, requiring fee-based permits and guides for all hunts. The tribe also has established the Horse Lake Mesa Game Park on 20,000 acres of steep and rugged wild lands ranging in elevation from 7,500 to 8,500 feet. Fishing is approved on seven reservation lakes and along the scenic Navajo River. All waters are stocked annually with rainbow, cutthroat and brown trout. Fish that measure more than 20 inches are common. A tribal fishing permit is required.

Two major events are scheduled each year and tourists are welcome. The Little Beaver Roundup, scheduled for the third weekend of July, is the key summer celebration of the Jicarillas. A Saturday parade, three-day rodeo, Indian dances and a carnival attract visitors. During the ceremonies, a young tribal brave is crowned Little Beaver. The tribe also selects a young maiden to oversee the ceremonies. In mid-September, the Jicarillas host the Stone Lake Fiesta. Apache families gather from throughout the region, setting up tepees and brush shelters. Campfires brighten the night. Footraces between the two tribal

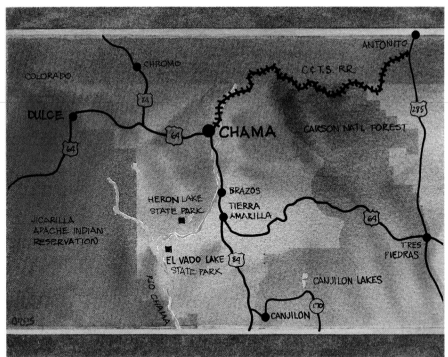

Top left—*Windsurfing at Heron Lake.* **Bottom left**—*A steam locomotive used by the Cumbres & Toltec Railroad.*

clans decide who will be more prosperous in the coming year. The race has been part of the Jicarilla culture for hundreds of years. There is no charge for tourists. The Jicarillas also invite visitors to join them in Saturday bingo at the Jicarilla Inn.

Chama. This far-north New Mexico town, lying at the foot of Cumbres Pass only nine miles from the Colorado border, takes its name from the Tewa language—*tzama*. Authorities differ over the word's exact meaning. Some say it means "here they have wrestled." Others say it means "red," and identifies the reddish water of the Chama River. No matter. This is truly a town carved out of the rough-and-tumble frontier days of the 1860s. Gunfights, hangings, hard-drinking trappers, cowhands and drifters marked an era of lawlessness typical of the Old West. As Eleanor Dagget notes in her book on Chama, necktie parties were common for horse thieves and others. Unmarked graves, where scoundrels were unceremoniously buried, are rumored to lie on the western edge of town now covered by homes.

This area once was heavily forested and boasted abundant game when the first white man traveled through. Crude log cabins were built in the early 1860s and, by 1865, a saloon, blacksmith and tent hotel comprised the town's chief structures. It grew as a stopover point on the wagon trail between the Ánimas Valley to the north and Santa Fe. But the land's natural beauty also held the promise of riches. By 1870 the first sawmill was set up and crews stripped the rolling countryside of trees south past what is now Tierra Amarilla and west to the Continental Divide.

In 1876 work was started on the Denver & Río Grande Railroad, a narrow-gauge line between Walsenberg, Colorado, through the San Luis Valley and then west to the Four Corners. It reached Chama in 1881, crisscrossing the border between New Mexico and Colorado. The line gave Chama a link to markets in Denver, Omaha and Chicago. As Dagget notes, ". . . the seemingly endless forests would be cut." Coal was found 18 miles west of Chama. Italian immigrants came in 1884 to dig for the black rock and named the mining community Monero, Italian for "money." The remains of Monero lie between Chama and Dulce on US 64. Old tailing piles and ramshackle shacks are an invitation to the explorer who uses common sense.

Seven years after the railroad entered Chama, forests within a range of 30 miles to the south and west had been exhausted. The endless forests were gone. Today, what was forest land is now rolling meadows. Ageless stumps occasionally can be seen from the road as cattle and sheep graze these man-made meadows.

Downtown Chama is a mixture of old and new. Some log buildings still can be seen. And the old Foster Hotel, across the street from the railroad, offers a glimpse into the region's historic past. While the town has had its economic ups and downs, the decision in 1974 between the states of New Mexico and Colorado to purchase 64 miles of the old railroad line between Antonito, Colorado, and Chama and restore the railroad's rolling railroad stock as a tourist attraction has put Chama back on the map.

The Cumbres & Toltec Railroad takes the visitor on a spectacular ride into the past. The coal-fired engines pull you through the scenic gorges of the southern Rockies, over high-mountain trestles and through tunnels blasted during another era. The line once linked boomtown mining camps scattered through the San Juan Mountains. It takes you over the rolling high country of southern Colorado, across the awesome Toltec Gorge and Los Pinos River, cresting at Cumbres Pass 10,015 feet above sea level before it drops down a 4-percent grade to Chama. The railroad is registered as a National Historic Site and has been in several movies.

Chama is a delightful old town to poke through. Many homes still in use were built to house railroad and sawmill workers. The adobe homes found 10 miles south in Tierra Amarilla, reflecting the traditional Hispanic culture, are out of place here. Log cabins and clapboard homes with pitched roofs are far more common. While some have fallen into disrepair, others are being restored as new economic life enters the community.

In the winter, Chama bills itself as the Snowmobile Capital of New Mexico. Snowfall is serious business; it's not measured in inches, but in feet. Wide, open meadows, forest service access roads and a variety of trails offer the snowmobile enthusiast miles of territory. Cross-country skiers also converge on the Chama area. The heavy snowpack, broad meadows and high ridges entice those who like to see this winter wonderland on "skinny skis."

The annual Chama Chile Classic is a five-kilometer and 10-kilometer cross-country ski race at Cumbres Pass. Skiers of all ages and abilities have turned the event into one of Chama's most successful winter festivals.

Each year more than 400 contestants gather at the crest of Cumbres Pass in February to race a tracked course through the high mountain meadows above Chama. As John Renna, one of the organizers explained, "This is a low-key race for everyone."

Besides skiing, logging and ranching, the economy receives a steady boost from hunters and fishermen who come to test their skills. Good elk and deer hunting is found on state lands and at private preserves. Trout fishing along the Chama River south of town seldom disappoints the serious angler. Well-kept commercial cabins complement the town's neat-as-a-pin motels, some boasting decor straight from the 1950s. Small family-style restaurants offer down-home cooking—fried chicken, chicken-fried steaks, mashed potatoes, pork chops and hamburgers—as well as traditional menus of New Mexican food.

For a few days in the summer of 1967, the remote village of Tierra Amarilla was in the national news. A small group called the Alianza Federal de Mercedes (Federal Alliance of Land Grants) led by Reies Lopez Tixerina raided the Rio Arriba County Courthouse to demand that land snapped up by the federal government in the early 1900s be returned to villagers. Three law officers were wounded and a deputy sheriff and an Associated Press reporter were abducted. Although the raid focused attention on the land problems of the north, land-grant ownership continues to be a legal Gordian knot. Today, the village of Tierra Amarilla looks much the same as it did 20 years ago. The courthouse still stands in the center of the village. Narrow streets and adobe structures testify to a continued reliance on the old ways.

North of Tierra Amarilla, just off US 84 in the old village of Los Ojos, a new enterprise is gaining national recognition. Tierra Wools, a nonprofit cooperative venture, is working to revitalize the area's traditional sheep and wool industry. The cooperative wants to preserve the best of New Mexico's Hispanic weaving tradition. Visitors can drop by the Tierra Wools showroom, headquartered in a century-old mercantile building in Los Ojos, and examine the beautiful handwoven goods that are for sale.

Continue through Los Ojos and follow the signs to the Parkview Trout Hatchery. The Department of Game and Fish welcomes visitors. A multimillion dollar renovation project is preserving these historic buildings and modernizing the hatchery facilities. A new visitor center will make a weekend visit an educational delight for the family.

Another spot to stop is the old Stone House Lodge at the north end of El Vado Lake. Take NM 95 west at the Rutheron-La Puente turnoff a few miles north of Tierra Amarilla. It is 14 miles from US 84 and 1 mile from Heron Lake. Built in 1935 by the Santa Fe Elks Club, the lodge is now owned and operated by Dell and Marilyn Morrison. While it has been modernized inside, the old stone structure still looks much as it did when first built. "We're thrilled to have people come look at it," said Marilyn Morrison. The lodge is frequently rented to large groups, particularly cross-country skiers. Recreational vehicle campsites also are found near Heron and El Vado.

The lakes offer the water enthusiast plenty of opportunity to fish, motorboat, sail or water-ski. El Vado is designated for power boats, while Heron Lake is classified as a slow-speed lake, making it ideal for sailors and fishermen in small craft. Campsites line the lakeshore. Additional information is available at the visitor center. During the summer, sailing regattas are conducted at Heron. El Vado hosts an annual fishing derby in June; Heron presents one in August. In late fall, when kokanee salmon spawn, fishermen are allowed to snag up to 24 per day. The salmon typically spawn at the age of four and then die. Hundreds of fishermen dot the shoreline or fish from boats to get their limit. Extremely cold winters will sometimes freeze the lakes to more than two feet in depth, making them ideal for ice fishermen. But park rangers urge caution when fishing on ice.

Dulce is the tribal center for the Jicarilla Apache Reservation. The reservation covers 750,000 acres of rugged wild lands and boasts abundant fish and game for the outdoorsman. Chama lies 26 miles east of Dulce and is headquarters for the famed Cumbres & Toltec Railroad. Chama is often called the Snowmobile Capital of New Mexico and hosts the Chama Chile Classic, a major cross-country ski race that attracts more than 400 contestants annually.

POPULATION: Dulce, 2,500. Chama, 3,000.

ELEVATION: The Jicarilla Reservation ranges in elevation from 6,500 feet to 9,000 feet. Chama: 7,860 feet.

CLIMATE: The average high temperature in July is 73 degrees with an average low at night of 37 degrees. In January the average high is 33 degrees with an average low of 3 degrees.

PRECIPITATION: Average annual snowfall ranges from more than 60 inches in Dulce to 75 inches in Chama with frequent summer thunderstorms.

SPECIAL EVENTS: In Dulce, the Little Beaver Roundup in July and the Stone Lake Fiesta in September. In Chama, the Chama Chile Classic, Balloon-Snowmobile Festival and winter festival in February. Sailing regattas at Heron Lake in June, July and August; annual burro and llama races in July.

NEARBY ATTRACTIONS: In Dulce, visit Indian ruins, Cedar Springs Lookout, the Jicarilla Apache Museum and Arts and Crafts Center and the Navajo River Bridge. Near Chama, see El Vado and Heron lakes, Tierra Wools, Parkview Trout Hatchery, Cumbres Pass and the Cumbres & Toltec Railroad.

Tres Hermanas, a trio of peaks standing close together, break the horizon south of Deming.

Mark Nohl

Deming & Lordsburg

by Cathy Caudle

Southwestern New Mexico is a land of peculiar contrast. Vast vistas of fierce grandeur stretch in seeming endlessness from the southernmost bootheel of Hidalgo County north to Grant County and east through Luna and Doña Ana counties. There is a gripping starkness evidenced here by the rocky Peloncillo and Pyramid mountains extending south from Lordsburg and in the rugged Floridas rising southeast of Deming.

It appears to be a lonely, empty land of timeless distance, barely scratched by the linking east/west gray turf of I-10. It is indeed a restless, windswept, barren land of ragged stone ridgelines. Desert mesquite, greasewood and creosote jutting up from caliche soil contribute to this impression.

Yet an ethereal quality accompanies this forbidding landscape. There is magic here, an enchantment that has something to do with the sky in all its seasons, with the gradations of light and earth hues that reflect off spectacular red-tiered canyons. It is in the late summer billowing of steel-gray thunderheads, and in the January pale blue meeting brown at horizon and in the fine-line silhouettes of windmills, yuccas and ocotillos against cool blue-pink pastel or fiery red-cloud sunsets. Even with no sound but the wind blowing through the native grasses, there is a closeness to life in this country, a gentle rhythm like the breathing of time, which can cause even the most harried vacationer to pause and reflect upon the immensity of the stillness and the simple beauty.

The traveler journeying east or west on I-10 between Tucson and El Paso might turn a casual eye and wry

The Great American Duck Race, above and right, attracts thousands to Deming each August. The event is the world's richest duck race.

smile on Deming, a town of 12,000 that at first glance appears to be in the middle of nowhere. Deming is in the center of Luna County, 59 miles west of Las Cruces, 50 miles south of Silver City and 60 miles east of Lordsburg. The rich and flavorful history of this small, modern city dispels the undermining limitations of such a stereotype and residents are proud to enlighten curious visitors.

Originally founded in October 1881 as New Chicago, Deming was a lawless town held by Winchesters and six-shooters. Where Southern Pacific and Santa Fe Railroad planners envisioned a great, booming metropolis, tents, shanties and boxcars housed wild ruffians beside the tracks. Warring factions from competing railroads caused many skirmishes, and several people were killed in cold blood as tent owners fought tooth and nail to keep sites and stakes. The whole community was abruptly relocated 10 miles east in late 1881 and the new site was christened Deming in honor of Mary Ann Deming, daughter of the Indiana man who industriously promoted the area for the Southern Pacific.

The early history of the Deming environs is as fascinating as that of any area in the Southwest. Fossils of prehistoric mastodons have been discovered in the sands of the Mimbres Valley, a land once peopled by the Mimbreño Indians, a vanished culture that produced unearthly and unequaled pottery. Scholars from all over the world come to study the remains of these ancient inhabitants whose life source was inexplicably caught up in the waters of the Río Mimbres, a mysterious river that disappears on the dry soil southeast of Deming after traveling hundreds of miles from the fertile Black Range in the north.

Early Spaniards made their impact on the area with treks into Mexico. The Florida (Floor-ee´-da) Mountains trace their name from these early discoverers. Embellished Las Floridas, in tribute to the colorful flora in the desert landscape according to one legend, the mountains join past and present with their solemn beauty.

The Goodnight-Loving cattle outfit set up a ranch in the Deming area in 1866 and other well-known ranches, such as the Diamond A and the Alamo Hueco, are now firmly established. Many area traditions have roots in cowboy heritage, including the practice of the *charivari,* or the serenading of a new bride and groom with cowbells. The discordant sounds of a *charivari* still sometimes fill the nights of wedding days.

Mark Nohl

Eduardo Fuss

Above—Rock Hound State Park, where visitors may go on treasure hunts for semiprecious stones.
Left—An exotic oryx at the Redrock Game Preserve and Wildlife Refuge north of Lordsburg.

Mid-1800s gold seekers heading for California camped here before the town came to be, and Civil War troops from Carleton's California Column chased Confederates south through the area back across the Río Grande. Warring Apaches watched in hostile silence, often astride horses with U.S. Cavalry brands, from nearby hills as soldiers from Forts McRae, Cummings and Craig grazed horses on the tall grass. The promontory knoll of Cook's Peak, rising 8,000 feet into the desert sky, watched in mute witness with surly, scoffing prospectors as Southern Pacific surveyors struck sources of plentiful and unusually pure water not 50 feet below the sun-dried ground. This discovery cinched Deming's future.

Morals were not at their peak in the frontier days between 1870-83. Saloons and gambling houses were the main businesses, and the lawless element did its best to maintain turmoil in the streets. When cowboys from outlying ranches were not coming in to raise the dust and hurrah the town, marauding Apaches raided to protest white settlers in their sacred valleys. From 1876-81 Indians accounted for 500 lives lost within a 50-mile radius of Deming. Eventually, a sense of civilization prevailed and by 1883 Deming became a more peaceful community. Churches replaced saloons and

a weekly newspaper (the *Deming Headlight*, named after a Southern Pacific engine) was founded.

Deming prospered as a railroad center and, for a time, was the only town with three depots of three independent railroads. The El Paso and Southwestern Railroad also used the busy tracks at Deming, and Phelps Dodge Copper Corporation ran a line from Deming to Bisbee, Arizona. The railroad became the focal point of the town's business. The Depot Hotel, a Harvey House, was one of the finest between Kansas City and San Francisco.

Today's visitor to Deming is invited to step into the nostalgia of the past with feet firmly rooted in the comforts and relative safety of the present. Visitors don't have to suffer the rigors of an all-day horseback ride to venture the few miles between settlements, nor do they have to wash the soot off after a train ride from Deming to El Paso. Yet the territory is still hauntingly similar to what it was 100 years ago.

Columbus, a village on the border with Mexico, is 30 miles south and a bit east of Deming on NM 11. In the early 1900s, nearby army camps were established because of border hostilities. On March 9, 1916, Columbus and adjacent Camp Furlong were attacked by about 1,000 Mexicans under the leadership of the infamous Pancho Villa. Twenty-nine American and 300 Mexican casualties resulted from this raid and, on March 10, 1916, President Wilson ordered Gen. John Pershing to lead an expedition into Mexico after Villa. It was the first time in American history that motorized vehicles and aircraft were used in warfare. At one point, the expedition penetrated as far as 516 miles into Mexican territory, not without difficulties, and managed to do some harm to Villa's forces. In early 1917, the Americans pulled out of the conflict because of pending trouble in Europe. Before this, full-scale occupation of Mexico was considered.

Today Columbus serves as a quiet haven for retirees and people seeking solitude. Southwest of the village is Pancho Villa State Park, created in 1959 in memory of the last hostile action by foreign troops within the continental U.S. Ruins of the original Camp Furlong, a state park museum, a desert botanical garden and views of Southwestern panoramas attract visitors. There are 61 campsites with water and electricity, two group shelters, a dump station, restrooms, showers and a visitors center. For more information, contact the Columbus Historical Society, PO Box 562, Columbus, NM 88029.

Rock Hound State Park, 14 miles southeast of Deming in the foothills of the Little Floridas, is situated on 250 acres of rugged gemstone and mineral-bearing terrain. The park offers 25 camping/picnicking facilities, a water system, playground equipment and sanitary facilities. Rocks and semiprecious stones are scattered on the slopes of the Little Floridas. Visitors may hunt for rocks and take them along when they leave. An annual Rockhound Roundup in March features more than 500 participants from 41 states. The Roundup offers guided rock trips (per pound fee charge), judging seminars and more. For more information, contact the Deming Gem and Mineral Society, Box 1459, Deming, NM 88031.

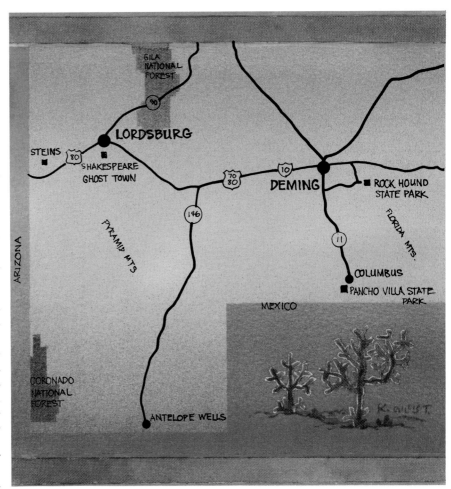

Mark Nohl

What started out as a brainstorming idea among a few Deming businessmen has escalated into the Great American Duck Race, otherwise known as the World's Richest Duck Race. Sporting a purse of $7,500, the late August race draws quackers from all parts of the country. Highlights include hot-air balloon races, the crowning of a Duck Queen and Duck Darling, the world's richest tortilla toss and other entertainment.

The Deming Luna Mimbres Museum, located in a building built by famous Southwestern architect Howard Trost, features Mimbres and other Indian relics, a wide assortment of gems and minerals and collections from bygone eras of the railroad and the rancher. A quilt room and a doll room add to the charm of the museum. Located at 301 South Silver Street, museum hours are daily 9-4, Sunday 1:30-4, closed holidays.

Deming also has a new Center for the Arts at 212 East Spruce. Art shows, musical concerts, poetry readings and theater workshops are among the activities, while a gift shop offers arts and crafts by local artists.

Sixty miles west and a world away from Deming on I-10 is the small city of Lordsburg, county seat of Hidalgo County. Lordsburg, like Deming, was officially established by the Southern Pacific Railway Company once sufficient water was discovered to meet the needs of a prospective community. In the days of railroad prosperity and mining booms, the area knew a period of wealth and renown beyond all expectations.

In early 1900, Samuel and Lee Wright and their sons hauled wood from Knight's Canyon to Lordsburg to generate the first electric lights known in that town. They drove as far as they could on Knight's Peak after firing the wood and joined with several ranchers to see the wondrous sight of the lights of Lordsburg.

In a similar community fashion, the first telephone line was strung in Lordsburg—on barbed wire. The line went from Mrs. W. H. Marble's residence to the ranch home of John Muir. The Arizona and New Mexico Railroad Company gave permission to use the top wire of its fences. The result was a perfect phone in dry weather. The barbed-wire line soon included eight neighboring ranches. J. E. Allen later installed a telephone system, connecting the barbed-wire line with a central office. Allen's lines were reported to be the best in the U.S. Whenever there was a concert in Lordsburg, Allen would ring people on the barbed-wire phone line, telling them to take down their phone receivers and listen. Then he would drop a receiver at the place of entertainment. The lines were later sold to the Bell Telephone Company.

There were a number of mining settlements near Lordsburg in the mid-1800s that have since passed into shades of memory. Many in their heyday overshadowed Lordsburg. Pyramid, also known as Leitendorf, once was a bustling camp with producing mines. Nine miles southwest of Lordsburg, Pyramid was a watering place and stage station on the Butterfield Overland Mail Company route for years. Another Butterfield point abandoned for lack of pure water was Steins, a bit south of Lordsburg, and yet another was Separ between Lordsburg and Deming. The most famous remaining remnant of the Butterfield Overland days is a ghost town once known as Mexican Springs, and also referred to as Grant, Ralston City, the Burro Mines and, finally, Shakespeare. Mexican Springs was a stopping place for California-bound adventurers, then a wild boom town relying on purportedly generous deposits of minerals in the surrounding mountains. From day one, the prosperity of the town fluctuated with the mining economy, and by 1932 the town was deserted. In 1935, Frank and Rita Hill purchased the abandoned Shakespeare and began to slowly restore the old buildings. They meticulously unearthed and preserved the history of the ghost town; today their daughter and her husband, Janaloo and Manny Hough, give guided tours of Shakespeare, generally the second and fourth weekends of each month at 10 am and 2 pm, the Houghs appear at their front gate in full 1800s regalia to guide interested people through their rustic home.

The old hotel where Billy the Kid washed dishes and the old Grant House dining room where Russian Bill and Sandy King were hanged still stand, much like they were then, restored authentically with dirt floors and yucca ceilings intact. The story of the lawless mining town is told, and bullet-pocked buildings stand in witness to the tales. Visitors marvel at the audacity of the diamond swindle of the 1870s and gawk at the nooses swinging silently in the breeze in the dining hall. No one curious about the history of southwestern New Mexico should miss this tour. A donation is requested to help maintain the buildings. For more information, contact Janaloo Hough, PO Box 253, Lordsburg, NM 88045 (542-9034).

Other Lordsburg attractions include the nearby Redrock Game Preserve and Wildlife Refuge on NM 464 north of Lordsburg. Visitors with binoculars or telephoto lenses stand a good chance of seeing bighorn sheep, deer and ibex. Hidalgo County also is one of the few spots in the country where javelina, or small wild pigs, can be hunted. Hidalgo County boasts some of the best quail hunting in the state.

More recent area attractions are wineries established in both Lordsburg and Deming. St. Clair Vineyards and Winery is on NM 549 three miles southeast of Deming. Two brothers, Vincent and Noel Vuignier, established St. Clair in 1984 in the Mimbres Valley. The Vuigniers bring their family's old-world wine-making traditions from Europe and combine them with ideal climate to produce New Mexico wines that rival the best anywhere. The St. Clair Sauvignon Blanc Reserve 1984 won a gold medal at an international competition in Geneva, Switzerland. The winery opens for tours and tasting. Call 546-6585 or write PO Box 112, Deming, NM 88031.

The Blue Teal Vineyards of the New Mexico Wineries is east of Lordsburg via exit 34 off I-10. The owners, the Lescombs family, have been in the wine-making business in Algeria and France. The Blue Teal brand is widely available in New Mexico. For tours and tasting, call 542-8881 or drop by the farm.

Wherever you end up in southwestern New Mexico, enjoy. This is the land of *poco tiempo,* and it is meant to be savored and enjoyed for its many scenic and cultural variations.

With its sunny climate, Deming has emerged as a growing retirement community and center for agriculture. Principal crops are cotton and feed grains. Deming offers easy access to Mexico via the Columbus/Las Palomas port of entry 30 miles to the south. Another gateway to Mexico is at Antelope Wells, 90 miles south of Lordsburg. Like Deming, Lordsburg attracts many retirees. The area economy also gets a boost from ranching and tourism.

POPULATION: Deming, about 12,000. Lordsburg, about 5,200.

ELEVATION: Deming, 4,335 feet above sea level. Lordsburg, 4,145 feet above sea level.

CLIMATE: In summer, the nights are in the mid to high 60s, with the days ranging into the mid and high 90s. Because of low humidity and prevailing westerly breezes, the hot summer days are pleasant. Temperatures will sometimes drop below freezing during the winter nights but rise into the mid and high 50s during the day. There is sunshine an average of 350-60 days a year.

PRECIPITATION: 8.5 inches annually.

SPECIAL EVENTS: The Rockhound Roundup at the Southwestern New Mexico State Fairgrounds in March; the Lordsburg Optimist Club Windsail races in April; in August, annual Hot-Air Balloon Festival in Lordsburg and the Great American Deming Duck Race; in the fall, the Southwestern New Mexico State Fair, Deming's Klobase Festival and the Lordsburg Arts and Crafts Fair.

NEARBY ATTRACTIONS: Rock Hound State Park, Pancho Villa State Park, City of Rocks State Park, the ghost towns of Shakespeare and Steins and the Redrock Game Preserve and Wildlife Refuge.

Mark Nohl

Rock Hound State Park in the Little Florida Mountains near Deming.

Shiprock west of Farmington.

Mark Nohl

Farmington

by Susan Hazen-Hammond

An ancient Navajo legend tells us that long ago a huge black bird appeared in the blue skies over the land now known as San Juan County. On its back it carried the People from the land beyond the setting sun. Landing in a field of orange flowers, the bird turned to stone, and the People—the Diné or Navajo—named it Tse-bida'hi, the Rock with Wings.

Today the legend-evoking Rock with Wings, better known as Shiprock, is just one of the spectacular attractions that lure travelers to the northwest corner of New Mexico, where the canyons, mesas and plains of Arizona, Utah, Colorado and New Mexico merge in right-angle boundaries. Every year thousands of visitors stop at the Four Corners Monument on US 160, the only place in the United States where four state corners meet. Besides the towns of Farmington, Bloomfield, Aztec and Shiprock, the tour includes colorful Navajo trading posts, a 15,000-acre lake, ancient Indian ruins, fertile high-desert farmland and picturesque badlands.

Farmington is the Hub of the Four Corners, at the junction of US 550 and US 64. Founded in the 1870s as—you guessed it—a farming town, the area bore a Navajo name meaning Three Waters, because the San Juan, Ánimas and La Plata rivers flow together here. Since 1950, Farmington has blossomed like a time-

Angel Peak area near Farmington.

lapse rose from a quiet village of 3,600 people to a quasi-metropolis (by New Mexican standards) of about 35,000 people. Agriculture still thrives, but the city's main economic base today is industrial, tied to the 11,000 wells that tap the vast oil and gas reserves in the San Juan Basin and to coal-fired power plants that consume 25,000 tons of coal a day.

Farmington makes an excellent base for exploring the surrounding countryside. The city's attractions include a municipal museum and a year-round assortment of special events: the Apple Blossom Festival in April, rodeos in May and June, a balloon rally Memorial Day weekend, a vintage auto Rod Run on the Fourth of July and the national Connie Mack World Series in August. The Cultural Heritage Festival in October features not only the three traditional New Mexico cultures—Indian, Hispanic and Anglo—but also food, entertainment and folkways from cultures and countries as diverse as Japan and Czechoslovakia.

Just east of town on US 64, between Bloomfield and Farmington, horse-racing fans gather on weekends from the end of April to the first of September at San Juan Downs to watch thoroughbred, Appaloosa and quarter horse-racing and to place wagers on their favorites.

The fields of blooming wildflowers around Bloomfield, 13 miles east of Farmington on US 64, give the area a radiant glow, but the town's name comes from an early settler named Bloomfield. Another settler, George Salmon, contributed his surname to Bloomfield's sightseeing highlight: Salmon Ruin, located two miles west of town on US 64. Nine centuries ago Indians now known as Anasazi (a Navajo name translated as Ancient Strangers) moved up from Chaco Canyon 50 miles to the south and built a carefully planned condominium-like town in the shape of a crescent.

Following principles of conservation archaeology, whereby ruins are preserved undisturbed for future investigators, archaeologists have excavated only about a third of the original 250 spacious, high-ceilinged rooms. Even so, more than 1.5 million artifacts were recovered, and emphasis today is on providing visitors with a sense of what it was like to live here in ancient times. The San Juan Archaeological Research Center at Salmon Ruin sponsors a wide range of programs including weaving classes taught by a Navajo weaver, fireside talks, moonlight walks and field trips.

From Bloomfield take NM 544 north to the All American City of Aztec, where other ancient ruins gave their name to the town. Early settlers, seeing the abandoned stone villages, concluded—entirely erroneously—that Aztec Indians must once have lived here. These mysteriously departed Indians, were, of course, the Anasazi, ancestors of today's Pueblo Indians. Their village ruins now are a national monument featuring a carefully reconstructed great kiva. For an interesting contrast, drive through the residential areas of the city of Aztec to see charming Victorian residences.

About 25 miles east of Aztec lie the shimmering blue waters of Navajo Lake. In good weather, take NM 173 east and NM 511 north. Otherwise, return to Bloomfield, and take US 64 to NM 511. At Navajo Lake State Park a 400-foot-high dam backs up the waters of the San Juan River to form a sparkling lake with 200 miles of fingered shoreline stretching into southern Colorado. A fisherman's paradise, these clear waters hold both warm- and cold-water fish. Water sport enthusiasts will enjoy opportunities for swimming, waterskiing and skin diving. Pine Site on the western side of the park and the

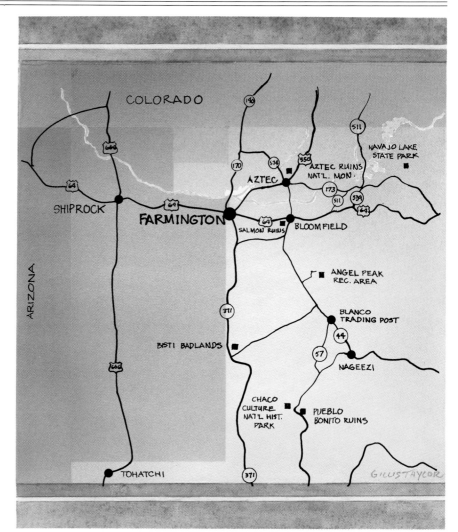

more primitive Sims Mesa Site on the eastern side both offer camping areas.

Colorful Navajo trading posts provide the next adventure in this region of diverse attractions. From Navajo Lake return to Bloomfield and take NM 44 south to the Blanco or Nageezi trading posts, (36 and 44 miles from Bloomfield, respectively) where you'll encounter a lively mixture of present and past, familiar and foreign. Brightly dressed Navajos, talking quietly in the distinctive Navajo language, wander up and down the crowded aisles of the trading post buying food and other goods. The trading posts also double as informal community gathering places.

If you're an adventurous bargain hunter who would

like to spend a weekend trip exploring some of the lesser-known trading posts that also sell beautiful handwoven Navajo rugs and other handiwork, the Four Corners area is ideal. The Farmington Convention and Visitors Bureau can give you a comprehensive list. For those traveling the roads between Farmington and Shiprock, you might plan a stop at the Hogback Trading Company in Waterflow on US 550, established in 1871, and the Fruitland Trading Post and Hatch Trading Post in Fruitland. The Carson Trading Post is a short 12-mile drive from Bloomfield on NM 44.

Both Blanco Trading Post and Nageezi serve as turning points onto dirt roads that lead to the most spectacular Anasazi ruins in New Mexico, the Chaco Cul-

Left—*Detail of Chaco Canyon's Pueblo Bonito ruin.* **Center**—*Ruins at Aztec National Monument.* **Right**—*Inside the restored Great Kiva at Aztec.*

ture National Historical Park. Park officials recommend taking the shorter road from Nageezi, which is less likely to turn into a slippery, muddy skating rink in the rain. It is best to call park headquarters (786-5384) for a road report. After traveling at 30 to 35 miles per hour along the 18 bumpy miles (from Nageezi; 24 miles from the Blanco Trading Post) of dirt road, you may wonder if this trip can really be worth it. For most of the approximately 50,000 visitors who travel here each year, the answer is a definite yes.

Nine centuries ago, Chaco Canyon served as the heart of a vast network of Anasazi villages linked by culture, custom, an elaborate system of roads, and perhaps political ties. Today the canyon contains more than a dozen major ruins and numerous smaller ruin sites. There is a small campground at Chaco, but no motels, gas stations or stores. Plan accordingly.

Stop at the visitor center to orient yourself to the park and to observe Anasazi artifacts such as "cloud blowers" and turquoise-inlaid hide scrapers. From the visitor center a paved loop drive leads to the major ruins, where massive stone walls and sturdy vigas once supported buildings up to five stories high. With poetic names such as Pueblo Bonito (pretty village) and Pueblo del Arroyo (village by the stream), these dramatic ruins offer insight into the culture and cus-

toms of the Indians of a millennium ago. Visitors with extra time and a spirit of adventure may hike on the mesas on both sides of the valley to explore other ruins and to see spectacular panoramic overviews.

Archaeologists still have many questions about Chaco Canyon and the Anasazi. Numerous theories attempt to explain why the Anasazi abandoned their stone homes in Chaco Canyon, never to return, about the year A.D. 1300 and to determine the exact role of Chaco Canyon in the Anasazi culture. For the average visitor, though, it's enough to know that not so long ago, as life on earth is measured, this dry desert canyon and the carefully constructed villages that now stand in ruin echoed with the sounds of human activity—laughter, cooking, eating, dancing.

Northwest of Chaco Canyon rise the colorful natural spires of the Bisti Badlands. For those with four-wheel-drive vehicles and a good sense of direction, the Bisti Badlands can be reached from Chaco Canyon from an unpaved and unmarked road. However, for most travelers the simplest way to reach the badlands is to return to Farmington from Chaco via Nageezi (or Blanco). Then from Farmington take NM 371 south to the Bisti.

Dramatic geological formations of sandstone, shale and clay offer eerie and breathtaking otherworldly

Bisti Wilderness Area south of Farmington.

scenes. Today dinosaur fossils, petrified logs and plant and animal life in 30,000 acres of the badlands are protected in two federally designated wilderness areas. The region also contains some of the richest coal deposits in the world. Long ago the Anasazi fashioned figurines, pendants and beads from the coal.

This tour could include a number of other stops for travelers who can spend more time in the area. For example, the Angel Peak Recreation Area six miles northeast of NM 44 is often compared to the Grand Canyon because of the beautiful weathered slopes in shades of red and lavender. The Farmington area is an ideal stopping place for those headed to Monument Valley or Canyon de Chelly. Four-wheel-drive enthusiasts will find they have almost unlimited terrain to explore. And 30 miles west of Farmington on US 64 lies the low-key Navajo town of Shiprock. Just south of town rises the famous 1,450-foot-tall Shiprock, Tse-Bida'hi (the Rock with Wings), which long ago brought the People here from the land beyond the setting sun.

Farmington's economy is based on mining, oil, tourism, construction and agriculture. It is the gateway to the Navajo Reservation. Farmington serves as the crossroads to a variety of recreational and tourist attractions—from the Indian ruins at Chaco Canyon and Aztec to the nearby southern Colorado mountains.

POPULATION: City, 31,222. County, 81,433.

ELEVATION: 5,395 feet above sea level.

TERRAIN: Mesa country with plateaus.

CLIMATE: Winters are chilly with temperatures of 43 degrees during the day and 17 degrees at night. Warm summer temperatures average 92 degrees during the day and drop to a cool nighttime average of 57 degrees.

PRECIPITATION: Annual average is 7.8 inches.

NEARBY ATTRACTIONS: San Juan Downs/ McGee Park, Chaco Culture National Historical Park, Navajo Dam Recreation Area, trading posts, Shiprock, Four Corners Monument, Bisti Badlands, Bolack Game Reserve and Wildlife Museum, Salmon Ruin, Angel Peak Recreation Area and the Navajo Reservation.

Eduardo Fuss

Gallup

by Ruth Armstrong

In the heart of New Mexico's Indian country near the Arizona border in western New Mexico, Gallup offers visitors a unique weekend experience. Few artists could match the bright palette of colors that delight the eye. Red, salmon, buff, pink and mauve cliffs and canyons dotted with splashes of green piñon and juniper surround Gallup under a vast turquoise sky. Ponderosa pine grows on the higher mesas, and a few miles away, mountain forests are broken with meadows and stands of aspens that in the autumn look as if molten gold flowed down the hillsides.

It's the people, though, who make this one of the most fascinating areas of the country. Gallup is the gateway to Indian country. The Navajo Reservation covers half the horizon north of town, and Zuñi Pueblo is 30 miles south. The superb crafts of both tribes fill shops and trading posts in Gallup. Even though they may be on city streets in modern buildings, they are authentic trading posts where Navajos and other Indians come to trade or sell sheep, wool, rugs, jewelry, pottery, kachina dolls and baskets for groceries, dry goods or cash. Inside, the Indians go deliberately about the serious business of buying and selling; outside they often squat in the shade of the store or by their pickups in sociable knots of conversation.

Gallup, a city of about 20,000, relies heavily on the

Overlook at El Malpais National Monument in the Grants area.

The map shows:

TOHATCHI

NAVAJO INDIAN RESERVATION

666

WINDOW ROCK

264

GALLUP

ARIZONA

RED ROCK STATE PARK

371

40 THOREAU

602

ZUÑI MNTS.

57

WHITEWATER

NUTRIA LAKE

BLUE WATER LAKE STATE PARK

ZUÑI PUEBLO

ZUÑI INDIAN RESERVATION

53

EL MORRO NAT'L. MON.

ZUÑI RIVER

tourist business that flows from I-40. In addition to serving as a trade center for the Navajos and Zuñis, at various times the town has been a business center for coal and uranium mines to the north and east.

Like many towns in New Mexico, Gallup is the product of the railroad-building era. As the main line of the Atchison, Topeka and Santa Fe Railroad pushed west, a railroad worker's camp was established there and named for the company paymaster. Rich coal deposits north of town gave it reason for permanency, and for a while it was called Carbon City. In the late 1940s when railroads began converting to diesel fuel, mines around Gallup began to close. In recent years coal has been strip-mined at several sites north of Gallup, but the town no longer depends on mining as its main economic base.

The biggest event in Gallup is the Inter-Tribal Indian Ceremonial in August. The first year, 1922, it was held in downtown Gallup, lighted by a circle of Model Ts with their headlights on. Later, ceremonial grounds were built, but when I-40 came through, it took the site. Since 1975 Red Rock State Park, 8½ miles east of town, has been home to the ceremonial. Buildings and bleachers built against the base and into the amphitheaters of huge red rock formations create a perfect backdrop for the spectacular ceremonial.

Opening night is always unforgettable. A Navajo medicine man and his sons enter the darkened grounds in a natural amphitheater against a steep cliff. The medicine man starts the sacred fire with sticks and tinder, then cleanses his hands in burning pitch. How he can do this without injury is part of the mystery and grandeur of this ceremony. Then the sons light torches in the sacred fire, which they use to start huge bonfires around the arena. Three young barefoot Navajos scale the cliff to plant flags of the Navajo Nation, New Mexico and the United States on top, their scramble up the cliff followed by spotlights.

The 14 or 15 dance groups that will perform in traditional costumes during the ceremonial and the parade through downtown Gallup on Saturday morning make a grand entry on opening night. Selected each year by a committee, they represent tribes from Florida to California and from Mexico to Canada. The colorful dances continue through the evening on Thursday, Friday and Saturday, and an all-Indian rodeo and sports events are in the afternoons.

On Sunday afternoon, the final day, both events are in the afternoon for the benefit of photographers. The rodeo, one of the largest Indian rodeos in the country, is sanctioned by at least three Indian cowboy associations. Participants come from all over the country, and all are professional.

The ceremonial showrooms and indoor and outdoor marketplaces open at 11 am daily and show the best in Indian arts and crafts. All items are for sale, and artists must be at least one-quarter Indian. Prejudging selects outstanding pieces to receive cash prizes.

The Red Rock Museum, open year-round, features exhibits on Zuñi, Hopi and Navajo cultures, prehistoric Anasazi and changing art exhibits. A one-hour videotape of the ceremonial can be viewed at the chamber of commerce office or at the visitor center.

The 16-million-acre Navajo Reservation lies about one-third in New Mexico and the rest in Arizona (except a small part in Utah). Several smaller separate sections, called the Checkerboard, are scattered across northwestern New Mexico. Window Rock, the capital, is 28 miles northwest of Gallup, barely across the Arizona border. The town backs up to a wall of red sandstone through which erosion has worn a large hole or window. Early in September each year, the Navajos gather for the Navajo Nation Fair, the world's largest American Indian fair. A rodeo, parade, pow-wow dancing, horse races, contests, food booths and arts and crafts exhibits add to the excitement, and the Miss Navajo Pageant selects a queen to reign for the following year.

Crownpoint, 60 miles northeast on the Checkerboard, is the site of the famous rug auctions sponsored by the Crownpoint Rug Weavers Association. Authentic Navajo rugs go on the block at the grade school about once a month on Friday evenings. (Contact the Gallup Convention and Visitors Bureau for dates.)

Zuñi, largest of New Mexico's 19 Indian Pueblos, lies 35 miles south of Gallup amid brilliant cliffs and canyons. This was the first pueblo seen by the Spaniards in 1540, when they were seeking the Seven Cities of Cíbola. They never found the fabled cities of gold, but they opened the Southwest to colonization and changed the face of the continent. Descended from the ancient farmers, the Anasazi, the Zuñis found their land was better suited for raising sheep and cattle, which they readily accepted from the Spaniards.

The Zuñis are best known for delicate jewelry that emphasizes intricately cut stones laid in silver. It may be purchased in an artists' co-op in the pueblo—check with Zuñi Tribal Headquarters for location. An ongoing project of the past dozen years has been the restoration of an old church dating back to the 1700s. Zuñi artist Alex Seowtewa and his sons are painting striking murals of Shalako kachinas and other Zuñi cultural symbols on the interior walls of the church. Shalako, a spectacular two-day Zuñi ceremony in late November or early December, is open to visitors if they abide by the rules—no photography, drinking or other disrespectful activity.

Turning east at Zuñi and continuing 25 miles on NM 53, El Morro National Monument, a sandstone mesa, stands like a battleship on the high, timbered plateau, a landmark on all early trails. Not only was it easily seen, but most important, on one side was a never-failing pool of fresh water. Inscriptions have been scratched into the sandstone cliff, beginning with prehistoric Indian petroglyphs. The earliest Spanish inscription was in 1605. From the visitor center a trail leads around the base of the cliff past the inscriptions, and another climbs to the top of the butte to ruins of a pueblo believed to have been the home of the Zuñis before they moved west to their present location sometime around the 14th century.

For the outdoor enthusiast, there are many great locations to pitch a tent or park a trailer in the area around Gallup. Red Rock State Park, open all year, offers 130 spaces for trailers, motor homes and campers as well as designated areas for tents. Besides offering the weary traveler a pleasant place to camp amid the red rocks, the park also is the site of numerous special events, such as the Inter-Tribal Indian Ceremonial, the Lions Club Rodeo, the Balloon Festival, the Square Dance Festival and the Shrine Circus. For more information write: Red Rock State Park, P O Box 328, Church Rock, NM 87311.

Just 20 miles east of Gallup in the Cíbola National Forest's McGaffey Recreation Area, travelers will find fishing, camping, hiking and picnicking at McGaffey and Quaking Aspen parks, open from April to October.

Navajo tribal officials welcome campers at designated areas throughout the reservation. They offer travelers a number of improved parks. A complete listing of camping fees and accommodations can be obtained by contacting the Navajo tribal offices in Window Rock, Arizona. Information on fishing permits required at many of the lakes is also available. Campers also will find a modern campground in Black Rock, just east of Zuñi. Tribal and state permits are required.

Farther away, but also enroute to Gallup, are camping areas at El Morro National Monument and at Bluewater Lake State Park, east of Gallup and closer to Grants.

There is too much to do and see in and around Gallup in one weekend, but one weekend will lead to another—and another. From the biting cold of a night at Shalako to the gentleness of a summer meadow near McGaffey Lake, from the trading posts in Gallup to the co-op in Zuñi, from the art exhibits at Red Rock State Park to the petroglyphs at El Morro, the contrast, the color, the people of this part of New Mexico are fascinating.

Gallup's economy is primarily based on tourism. The city also serves as the market center for 120,000 people who live in the surrounding area. Gallup is the county seat of McKinley County and serves as the gateway to three Native American reservations: Navajo, Hopi and Zuñi. Located on I-40 between Albuquerque and Flagstaff, Gallup has a long-established reputation for authentic Indian jewelry and arts and crafts.

POPULATION: Approximately 20,000.

ELEVATION: 6,500 feet above sea level.

TERRAIN: Redrock mesa.

CLIMATE: Temperature ranges are often extreme. There are four definite seasons. Humidity is generally low. January temperatures range from 43 degrees during the day to 1 degree at night. In July the high is about 87 degrees with a low of 53 degrees.

PRECIPITATION: Annual average is 10.7 inches.

SPECIAL EVENTS: Inter-Tribal Indian Ceremonial in August, Lions Club Rodeo the third week of June, Red Rock Balloon Rally in early December, Square Dance Festi-Gal in May and Mountain Men Rendezvous in mid-February.

Ácoma Pueblo west of Albuquerque.

Photography by Mark Nohl

Grants

by Emily Drabanski

I magine dropping down into a mine shaft, boating on a sparkling blue lake, exploring a lava tube, climbing down ancient sandstone steps from a mesatop Indian pueblo or feeling the chilling air from an ice cave. It sounds like something Walt Disney would have created. But it's all part of the natural handiwork you'll find when you visit the Grants area for a weekend trip.

Disney would have reveled at the sight of the rich crimson, maroon and lavender bluffs that rub against the turquoise sky in the Grants area. But it was a dusty, yellow rock that changed Grants forever.

That rock, of course, was uranium. You can learn more about the discovery of uranium by Paddy Martinez and the boom and bust cycles of the uranium industry when you visit the New Mexico Museum of Mining at 100 Iron Street in Grants. The shiny new museum is the city's showplace and also houses the chamber of commerce—a good place to begin your Grants weekend. Located off West Santa Fe Avenue, the main thoroughfare in Grants, you can't miss it. Look for the huge, painted drill bit and towering headframe next to the museum.

"Some folks say I spent 32 years preparing for retirement," Wayne Dolezal, a museum tour guide, said as a wide smile spread across his face. He doesn't miss uranium mining at all. But he is proud of his former profession and enjoys telling folks what it was like when he worked in the mines.

He rings bells to signal that a group is ready to descend in the "cage." Students and tourists squeeze into the elevator that takes them into a cool, dim underground world known as Section 26. "Everything down here is authentic to the last detail," Dolezal says as he leads the group deeper into the drifts (mining tunnels). Dynamite dangles from the walls, while the long hole drilling machine and other equipment take on an eerie glow.

"This looks just like the lunchroom where we ate everyday except we always had cockroaches," Dolezal says as the group crams into a tiny wood-floored room with a picnic table. But you don't have to worry about seeing cockroaches in this lunchroom. It's so clean that the museum welcomes groups to use it for fundraisers. Afterhours, people often nibble on hors d'oeuvres in this underground room.

Wearing his bright yellow Shiftless Sam the Prospector T-shirt, Dolezal talks with optimism for his hometown. Today, just a few years after the uranium industry's largest bust, most of those who've stayed are committed to getting Grants back on its feet.

Grants is surrounded by several outstanding tourism destinations. It's in the heart of Indian country, with both Ácoma and Laguna pueblos just a short drive east. The Navajo Nation lies to the west and Zuñi Pueblo is about two hours southwest of Grants.

The entire area is marked by ancient footpaths of the Anasazi Indians, who lived in Chaco Canyon, and their descendants. These ancient ruins at El Malpais will be linked with other ancient sites in New Mexico and Arizona by means of the Masau Trail, actually a trail using public roads along a tour route.

Located just minutes from Grants is one of the most diverse landscapes in the state—El Malpais (the badlands). In January 1988, 114,000 acres of this area of past volcanic activity were designated as El Malpais National Monument, with 262,000 additional acres set apart as a national conservation area to protect important archaeological, biological, recreational and historical resources. Two new Wilderness Areas are in the El Malpais National Conservation Area.

A loop road encircles the entire region. Large stretches are paved, but the loop's inner portion is unpaved, sometimes impassable in inclement weather. Depending on how much time you have and your sense of adventure, you can spend a few hours or several days in the area.

Most visitors use NM 117 off of I-40 and return by that route. This short drive introduces you to El Malpais. As you head south on NM 117, you'll see the Upper McCarty's lava flow on your right. It's the youngest—maybe as young as 1,000 years old. About 10 miles down the road, the Sandstone Bluffs Overlook offers a breathtaking eagle's-eye vista of the badlands. If you're out for a day's drive, this is the ideal place to stretch your legs on a hike or stop for a picnic lunch.

About five miles farther, you'll see a sculptured sandstone formation known as La Vieja (the old woman). Two miles beyond La Vieja is New Mexico's largest natural arch. A path leads to La Ventana (the window), which is now part of the new Cebolla Wilderness Area. This striking formation takes on different appearances with the changing light on the striated curve, turning it from a pale beige to a rainbow of earth tones. Just past La Ventana, you'll find yourself in the Narrows, so called because lava flowed to the base of the sandstone cliffs. A picnicking and camping area lies three miles beyond this area. This is the point where most people turn around and return to the interstate.

If you go farther, you can hook up with NM 53 along County Road 42, the dirt road that leads to the Chain of Craters region. The road can be rough and is unmarked. If you're unfamiliar with the territory but would like to explore the backcountry, contact Los Amigos del Malpais (the Friends of the Badlands). The Grants-based group knows this area and will take groups to explore the backcountry—lava tubes, archaeological ruins and ice caves. You can contact members at 285-5041.

Steve Fischer, El Malpais coordinator for the Bureau of Land Management, frequently leads excursions through El Malpais. The west side is a totally different world. Tall pines and junipers protrude like pinnacles out of this rough terrain. The Hawaiians came up with the terms to describe the types of lava found. The black, ropy type is called *pahoehoe*, while rough, broken lava is called *aa*. Fischer smiles and says a good way to remember the difference is to think of what you might say as you travel across this area in bare feet— ah, ah!

Since you have to walk across this rugged *aa* to reach the lava tubes in the backcountry, you need sturdy hiking boots—the terrain resembles a tray of broken brownies. Watch your step—deep crevices and loose pieces of lava can make you lose your footing. It's not

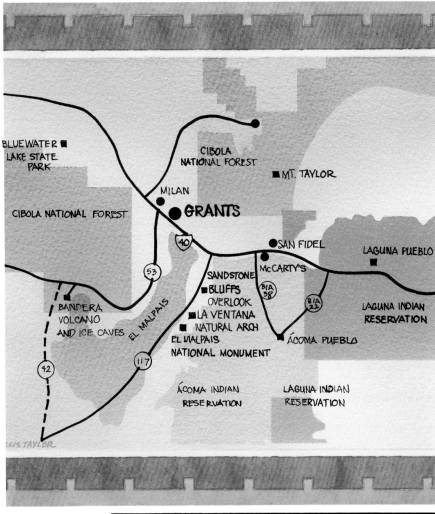

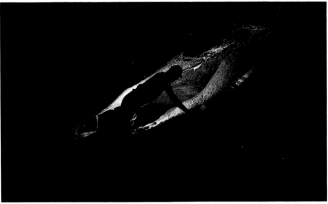

a barren land. Cacti bloom and animals scurry across this surreal forest floor.

One of the highlights of the backcountry is a 17-mile lava tube. A guide can help you find a collapsed section where you can reach the bottom of the tube by scrambling down littered volcanic boulders. Streaks of sunlight dance across the broken lava chunks dappled with orange and green lichen. The lava tubes formed when the outer surface of a lava flow cooled and hardened, while a raging hot river of molten lava flowed inside. Eight of these tubes mark the terrain.

The dirt road loops back to NM 53, but most tourists exploring the east side of El Malpais will come directly from NM 53 off I-40. This scenic route will take you past several El Malpais sites and lead you to El Morro National Monument and Zuñi Pueblo.

Volcanoland. That's what it says on David Candelario's cap and sign for his privately owned ice cave and crater. Candelario and his wife, Reddy, have run this spot for about 40 years. For an admission fee you can follow trails to an easily accessible ice cave. As you descend the wooden steps, you can feel the nip of ice-cold air rush out from this cave in a collapsed lava tube. A solid sheet of blue green ice glistens on the floor and delicate crystals and an occasional icicle spire cling overhead. This is one of many ice caves in El Malpais. Others are more spectacular, with large icicle stalagmites and intricate ice crystals, but are more remote and require ropes and other equipment for access.

Also in Candelario's Volcanoland is a trail to Bandera Crater, the largest cinder cone in El Malpais.

Looking into this lava cone in such close proximity to the ice caves, you can easily understand why this area is often called the land of fire and ice. "NASA did a survey out here and they told me this land was more like the moon than any other place on earth," Candelario said.

The entire El Malpais area is rich with history as well as geological wonders. Ancient trails mark this area containing several archaeological ruins. The first Europeans known to cross El Malpais were Capt. Hernando de Alvarado and Fray Juan Padilla in 1540 as they led a band of soldiers sent by the Spanish conquistador Coronado to explore the area east of Zuñi Pueblo. They were quick to report the roughness of the terrain, convincing Coronado to avoid the lava flow.

If you continue west on NM 53, you'll reach El Morro National Monument, where many travelers left their mark hundreds of years ago inscribed into the soft sandstone on what is often referred to as Inscription Rock. In April 1605, two years before the founding of Jamestown, Don Juan de Oñate left his inscription. Long before his arrival, hundreds of Indians had left petroglyphs on nearby rocks.

The El Morro visitor center offers a good introduction to the area's history. From the center, a self-guided tour will lead you to the base of a cliff to see the inscriptions and on to the top of a mesa with pueblo ruins. There's a picnic area and small campground at the monument.

Zuñi Pueblo is just a short drive from El Morro National Monument farther west off NM 53. Zuñi, the largest of the 19 pueblos, was the first pueblo seen by the Spaniards when they were seeking the Seven Cities of Cíbola. They never found the legendary gold, but you'll find fine examples of inlaid jewelry. The Zuñis also are known for their fetishes—stones carved into animal forms.

The pueblo church dates back to the 1700s. Zuñi artist Alex Seowtewa and his sons are painting murals of Shalako kachinas and other cultural symbols on the walls inside.

From Zuñi you can either drive to Gallup via NM 602 or return to Grants.

Two other pueblos are near Grants. If you're coming from the east out of Albuquerque on I-40, stop at Laguna Pueblo first. Keres-speaking Indians live in this large pueblo that maintains its original hilltop site.

Flanked by nearby purple and pink cliffs and buttes, the picturesque pueblo is visible from I-40. Outstanding amidst the jumble of traditional adobe homes is the pure, white church that reflects the sun off the hilltop.

The San José de la Laguna Mission was built around 1706 and acquired its distinctive white finish in 1977. Paguate Reservoir is open for fishing by permit available at the Laguna Police Office.

Just a short drive farther west on I-40, you'll reach the Ácoma exit at BIA Road 22. It's a short, scenic drive to the pueblo visitor center as you pass through green valleys dotted with sheep. Wind and weather have shaped the surrounding bluffs into fairy castle shapes.

The visitor center offers a museum, snack bar and gift shop. For a fee, a guide will take visitors on a shuttle to the top of Sky City, the mesatop home for the Ácomas for almost a thousand years. Today, most of the Ácomas live on farms and ranches and in the villages of McCarty's and Acomita. But their families maintain homes atop the mesa for feast days. Several families live there year-round to help maintain the church and guide visitors. Other families come to sell the distinctive black-on-white pottery.

The guides are friendly and eager to answer questions about their pueblo. You'll learn that there is no running water or electricity in the Sky City. Water for cleaning is collected from several natural collection pools.

A visit to the San Estevan Mission church highlights the tour. No photography is allowed inside, but the memory you can take will linger for years to come. Note the nine-foot-thick wall as you pass through the original ponderosa pine doors. This massive structure was built more than 350 years ago, taking the people 20 years to erect. They hauled large ponderosa pine timbers from Mount Taylor to the top of this mesa for the vigas that support the roof. One can imagine the stamina it took to carry these up the narrow, steep, sandstone stairsteps that led to the top of the mesa. The interior has beautiful, hand-painted Indian designs as well as a carved wooden saint and animal hide paintings. The exterior white finish and dual bell tower are all marks of this distinctive church's classic design.

After your guided tour, you may continue to browse at the pottery stands. Today, more families are dependent on the sale of pottery for their income as many pueblo residents have lost their jobs as miners. Most families still produce traditional pottery, although some make pots from molds. The best pots are thin and well shaped with classic designs painted on with a yucca brush. Some feature the distinctive scalloped fingernail imprints. You'll find prices are less expen-

Top—Atop the Sandstone Bluffs Overlook, the visitor can see for miles across El Malpais. ***Bottom, left***—A hedgehog cactus blooms amid black ropelike lava called pahoehoe. ***Bottom, right***—A carpet of moss and lichen covers boulders inside a lava tube in El Malpais.

Right—Light continuously changes the color of the Sandstone Bluffs Overlook at El Malpais.

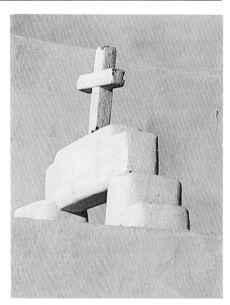

Left—*Detail of San José Mission at Laguna Pueblo.* ***Right***—*The center of Laguna Pueblo rests on a hillside visible from I-40.*

sive when you buy directly from the potter. And you can meet the artisan to ask questions about the design and the pot itself.

Your guide will take you back on the shuttle to the visitor center or if you're feeling more adventurous, you are permitted to walk down the well-worn sandstone steps that lead to the bottom of the mesa. In places the passageway is steep and narrow, but the views are well worth the effort. If you're heading back to Grants, go east through McCarty's village to get back to I-40.

For those seeking a weekend of fishing and boating, a trip to Bluewater Lake is highly recommended. The name is not misleading. This sparkling jewel surrounded by piñon- and juniper-studded hills in Bluewater Lake State Park offers great trout and channel cat fishing. Campgrounds, picnic areas and a marina hug the lake. Anglers also frequent this lake in the winter for ice fishing. Bluewater Lake State Park is near Prewitt, west of Grants off I-40.

If you return to I-40, you can head to Thoreau, where you can pick up NM 371 to go to Crownpoint for its famous Navajo rug auctions or continue on to Chaco Culture National Historical Park. Gallup is another popular destination en route to Arizona along I-40.

After a bust in its once prosperous uranium mining industry, Grants now is in the process of rebuilding and diversifying its economy. The surrounding natural geological formations make this a scenic destination for travelers. Extinct volcanoes, ice caves and sandstone bluffs are among the attractions. Several Indian pueblos are within easy driving distance of Grants—Ácoma, Laguna and Zuñi.

POPULATION: 11,900.

ELEVATION: 6,460 feet above sea level.

CLIMATE: July temperatures fluctuate from an average of 85 degrees during the day to 51 degrees at night. In January daytime temperatures average 49 degrees during the day and 15 degrees at night.

PRECIPITATION: 9.56 inches annually.

SPECIAL EVENTS: Mount Taylor Winter Carnival and Quadrathlon in February, Cíbola Day in June, a Fourth of July celebration with three rodeos, Bi-County Fair and Rodeo on Labor Day Weekend.

NEARBY ATTRACTIONS: Grants Mining Museum, Bluewater Lake State Park, El Malpais National Monument, Ácoma Pueblo, Laguna Pueblo, Zuñi Pueblo, El Morro National Monument and Mount Taylor.

A cowboy and his horse form a silhouette against the sunset north of Clovis.

High Plains

by Wendell Sloan

W hile other parts of the state speak loudly with snow-capped mountains or Indian crafts seen across the nation, east-central New Mexico speaks with the subtle whisper of a prairie breeze.

Driving through the oblong triangle from Fort Sumner, northeast to Tucumcari, then south through Clovis and Portales, the traveler can experience the nostalgia of the Old West, water-ski in clear lakes, camp out by shifting sand dunes, catch the sounds of bucking bulls in live rodeos, marvel at hot-air balloons ascending into the skies or watch comedies and dramas in indoor and outdoor theaters.

The Old West begins in Fort Sumner with the Billy the Kid Museum on US 60/84 two miles east of downtown. Billy the Kid, the infamous gunslinger, was shot and killed by Sheriff Pat Garrett in the dark of night on July 14, 1881, in a bedroom of the Pete Maxwell home—formerly the officers' quarters at Fort Sumner. The Billy the Kid Museum contains more than 60,000 relics of the Old West collected over many years by the late Ed Sweet. The exhibit includes old cars, such as a 1929 Model T Roadster and a 1923 Dodge Commercial Delivery. A reproduction of the tombstone of Billy the Kid, as well as a settler's shack, is located on the museum grounds.

Another attraction is the Old Fort Sumner Museum on NM 212, four miles south of US 60/84. The fort was originally authorized in 1862 to control 400 Mescalero Apaches and 8,570 Navajos who were uprooted from their homes during Col. Kit Carson's campaign against Indians in New Mexico. At its peak, Fort Sumner had a garrison of 600-700 infantry and cavalry troops. After an experiment to turn the Indians into farmers failed and after many had died or escaped, the

Indians were allowed to go home in 1868. In 1869 the army sold the fort for $5,000 to Lucien B. Maxwell of Cimarron.

The Old Fort Sumner Museum houses artifacts, pictures and historic documents. Behind the museum is the grave of Billy the Kid, as well as those of Lucien B. Maxwell and his family.

Just to the west is Fort Sumner State Monument. Displays in the monument building tell the story of Fort Sumner, with rangers on hand to answer questions. The monument is open daily.

For mural lovers, the top floor of the De Baca County Courthouse contains a series titled *The Last Frontier* by Texico artist Russel Vernon Hunter. Done under federal sponsorship in the 1930s, the murals depict families moving onto claims, the coming of barbed wire, the railroad, Billy the Kid and the beginning of Fort Sumner.

For water enthusiasts, Sumner Lake State Park lies 16 miles northwest of Fort Sumner. The 1,000-acre park features campground and cabin sites. The westside cabin area is a popular retirement community and weekend retreat. Tame deer often drop by for a free supper.

The park has four launching ramps for boats, tennis courts, a nature trail and playground. Sunbathers who prefer some privacy can pick an isolated stretch of shoreline and lie next to the water on warm, huge rocks.

Many warm-water fish can be found in the lake, including bass, catfish and crappie. Winter trout fishing is popular at the stilling basin below Sumner Lake Dam.

The trip northeast to Tucumcari on NM 209 offers a stark contrast in geography. After driving through miles of level, yucca-strewn ranching land, about 11 miles south of Tucumcari you suddenly encounter the Mesa Redonda—a series of hills jutting out of the prairie. Make sure your brakes are in good shape —it is a natural amusement park that will turn your car into a roller coaster.

Tucumcari looms in the Llano Estacado (staked plains) like an unexpected oasis for travelers. With two lakes within 32 miles of this town of 8,500, the cup runneth over for those interested in water recreation.

New Mexico's second-largest lake, Ute Lake, lies 25 miles northeast of Tucumcari and Conchas Lake is 32 miles northwest of town. They offer a plethora of water activities, including fishing, boating, swimming

and camping. Electric hookups, toilets and showers are available. Conchas Lake also has a lighted airstrip and a golf course in the vicinity.

Quay County is well known for its hunting, with plentiful deer, quail, doves, geese, ducks and antelope. The county offers some of the best blue quail hunting in the nation.

The Ladd S. Gordon Wildlife Area at Tucumcari Lake provides refuge for green-backed herons, pied-billed grebes, mallards, redheads and ruddy ducks. A. L. Gennaro, an Eastern New Mexico University biologist, says the lake is the only place in New Mexico where nests of the white-faced ibis have been sighted. The lake holds carp, bluegill and channel catfish.

As you travel back into Tucumcari across the short-grass prairie country broken by red clay, you can see herds of antelope galloping off in the distance like oversized jackrabbits.

Back in Tucumcari, take time out to visit the Tucumcari Historical Museum. Located four blocks from US 66, the museum contains thousands of items, including Indian artifacts dating to 12,000 B.C., a barbed wire collection, an early-day still and a 1900 windmill.

The Piñata Festival in June includes a crafts show, antique car show, Prince Tocom and Princess Kari contest for four- and five-year-olds, bike and trike races, pet races and a 100-mile bike tour. The festival concludes with a colorful parade representing the multicultural diversity of New Mexico.

Visitors to the area will also want to stop by the Caprock Amphitheatre, an outdoor theater 10 miles south of I-40 (Exit 356) at San Jon.

As the traveler approaches Clovis from Tucumcari on NM 209, huge silver contraptions spew water on a thirsty land. These irrigation sprinklers, drawing water up from the huge Ogallala aquifer, turn the dry land into a vast ocean of green crops.

In 1907 Clovis was known as Riley's Switch—a siding and a few rough shacks were all that were there. But when railroad officials made the spot the division point for the Belén cutoff, they decided to give the town a proper name. They chose Clovis, king of the Franks, whose conversion to Christianity in A.D. 496 changed the course of the Christian religion. Today, the railroad remains the largest private employer in Clovis.

Clovis' most festive occasion is Pioneer Days, celebrated in June. Pioneer Days began in 1935 as a gesture of defiance toward the Depression. A crowd of 15,000

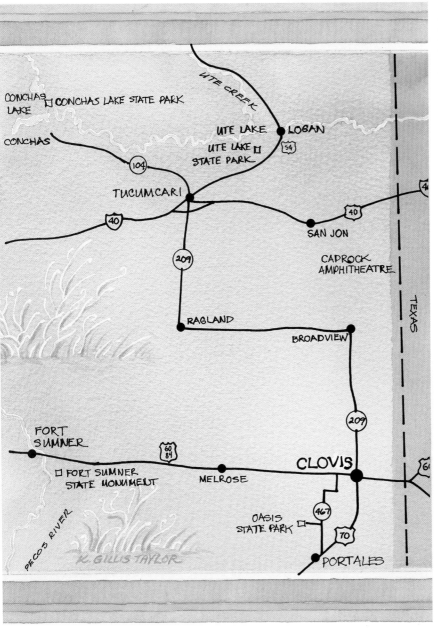

Animal lovers should stop by the Hillcrest Zoo in Clovis, west of downtown on Sycamore Street. The 22-acre zoo boasts more than 200 animals, including an elephant as well as a children's petting zoo.

Drama enthusiasts will want to make reservations at the ornate Lyceum Theatre, 411 Main Street. Originally built in 1919, the theater was closed in the '70s but now is open again.

Clovis offers 27 holes of golf—18 at the Colonial Park Country Club north of Clovis and 9 at the Municipal Course at 1220 Norris. Colonial Park Country Club has attracted some notoriety as the home of Mississippi kites, birds that swoop down at golfers to protect their nests. The birds have been successfully dislodged from the course by placing models of nests in the trees; the kites will not make their nests too closely to other nests.

Visitors in Clovis in August can enjoy the Curry County Fair. It features the usual rides, booths and activities plus large agricultural exhibits. While in town, visitors also may want to stop by the Ned Houk Park and Museum just north of Clovis.

Buddy Holly fans can learn the real Buddy Holly story by visiting the Norman Petty Studios at 200 Main in Clovis. The old studio a 1313 W. Seventh is open by appointment. Violet Petty, widow of Norman Petty, keeps the studio where Holly recorded some of his biggest hits. By the way, Mrs. Petty played the piano and celesta on Holly hits "Think It Over" and "Everyday." Those wishing a tour of the studios can call 763-7206.

Another little-known area attraction is the El Cid cutting-horse facility, owned by Lonnie and Barbara Allsup of Allsup's Convenience Stores, located on the New Mexico-Texas border north of Farwell. El Cid fea

gathered for the first parade, rodeo and dance. From its beginning, Pioneer Days celebrated good times. It has grown to include a balloon fiesta, beauty pageant, chile cook-off, the Clovis Mile, a rodeo, fiddlers' contest, antique car show, soccer tournament and country music festival.

Right—*A farmer tends his windmill near Clovis.*

tures cutting-horse competitions. It has a 2,000-seat outdoor arena, with plans for a 5,000-seat indoor arena.

While making the 20-mile trip south on US 70 from Clovis to Portales, you're apt to see greenish or silvery aircraft streaking unusually low and fast overhead. The planes are from Cannon Air Force Base, which represents a $256 million boost to the area economy. Cannon's 27th Tactical Fighter Wing is equipped with F-111Ds, the Air Force's most advanced fighter. The base employs about 3,750 military personnel and 800 civilians. The annual open house is in June.

As you continue to Portales, leaving the jets streaking behind over cotton and grain fields, you will pass a sign pointing toward Oasis State Park. Here you can relax among shady cottonwoods standing watch over shifting sand dunes, as campers and picnickers fish leisurely in a small, deep blue body of water.

Entering the Portales Valley, you will pass an orange and brown billboard that reads: "WELCOME TO PORTALES: A Town of 12,000 Friendly People . . . (and three or four old grouches)."

You can immediately see why Roosevelt County is called The Peanut Capital of the World. The rich, green peanut plants grow everywhere—usually to the tune of about 12,000 acres per year. The Portales Valley is the only important commercial producer of Valencia peanuts west of the Mississippi.

Peanuts are such an important part of the county's economy that Eastern New Mexico University hosts an annual Peanut Festival the third weekend in Oc-

tober. In addition to peanut-related foods and products, the festival features the Peanut Olympics—a series of humorous but competitive events such as peanut tossing at a bucket and peanut racing, in which contestants have to nudge a peanut with their noses across the finish line. The Peanut Festival also features more than 100 arts and crafts booths, square dancing, country music, gunfights and country-flavored entertainment.

Portales grew up around Portales Spring and matured into a full-fledged community in 1934 with the founding of ENMU. Bathed in hues of green grass and multicolored flowers, the 393-acre campus stands as an intellectual oasis in the heart of east-central New Mexico.

ENMU provides such cultural activities as mainstream and experimental plays, chorale groups, a symphony orchestra, country and rock concerts, football and basketball games, comedians and controversial speakers. It also operates three major museums: Blackwater Draw, the Roosevelt County Museum and the Natural History Museum.

Eastern New Mexico University, the third-largest college in the state, serves as the focal point for cultural activities in Portales.

Discovered in 1932 by A. W. Anderson of Clovis, Blackwater Draw is one of the most significant archaeological sites in North America. Groups that have funded or participated in research at the site include the Carnegie Institute, Smithsonian Institution, Academy of Natural Sciences, National Science Foundation and National Geographic Society, along with seven major universities.

The Folsom Point or Clovis Point spearheads found at the site represent the oldest evidence of man's existence in the new world. The site was first occupied by man about 10,000 years ago. It then was near a large pond fed by the headwaters of the Brazos River. The pond dried up some 7,000 years ago. Early investigations at Blackwater Draw recovered evidence of woolly mammoth, camel, bison, saber-toothed tiger and the dire wolf. In conjunction with the archaeological site, ENMU operates Blackwater Draw Museum on US 70 about seven miles north of Portales.

Roosevelt County Museum can be found on campus. The museum's artifacts tell the story of eastern New Mexico from the late 19th and early 20th centuries. Among the oldest items on display is an 1896 Sears Catalogue. Also on display are several governors' memorabilia, old dolls, a manual telephone switchboard used in Tucumcari in 1917, a square grand piano (circa 1840-1920), an 1899 American Type Founders Company Printing Press, firearms such as an 1819 Wafenfabruk and a Springfield Long Rifle, Indian artifacts, old school furniture and World War II souvenirs.

The paralyzing buzz of rattlesnakes is the first sound greeting those entering ENMU's Natural History Museum, open free to the public. Fortunately, the rattlers are safely enclosed behind glass cages, as is a 50-pound Burmese python snake. Other exhibits, live or stuffed, include an alligator, golden eagle, buffalo, great-horned owl, prairie dog, porcupine, a mongoose with its mouth wrapped around a cobra, native New Mexico fishes and an assortment of other creatures.

Art connoisseurs will want to view a mural representing the 12th chapter of Ecclesiastes painted on the stairway walls inside the ENMU Administration Building. It was painted under the Public Works Progress Administration by Albuquerque/Taos artist Lloyd Moylan. For five months Moylan and his assistant scaled the walls painting the mural. Government officials who inspected the work informed ENMU officials that it was "one of the most beautiful murals in any public building in the United States."

The Administration Building itself is worth a visit. Built in Old English style, only two-fifths of it could be completed with the funds originally available. On June 4, 1934, the school opened as Eastern New

Conchas Lake west of Tucumcari has become one of the state's most popular playgrounds. Fishing and boating are supplemented by hunting and golfing on a course next to the lake.

Mexico Junior College with 165 students attending classes in the partially completed building. Today, the 40-plus building campus serves more than 3,700 students. Branch campuses are located in Clovis and Roswell.

One of the eye-catching attractions in Portales is Bill Dalley's windmill collection, south of the city cemetery on Kilgore Street. Dalley has restored several antique windmills. A drive past his house reveals several standing, with many others in various states of repair. Dalley's windmills range from those with wood sails to those with metal; some have vanes and others do not. One of the most interesting looks like a miniature lighthouse. Of course, hundreds of windmills, many still in actual operation, can be seen throughout east-central New Mexico.

Just like its neighbors, Roosevelt County is a well-known hunting area. It is one of the few places in the world that offers great hunting for prairie chicken. Shotgun enthusiasts will also enjoy pheasant, quail and dove hunting. Ducks, geese and sandhill crane, which require federal stamps to hunt, are also plentiful.

The Grulla Wildlife Refuge, a (usually) dry salt lake, is east of Portales on NM 88. It is home to migratory birds, such as the sandhill crane, ducks and geese.

Clovis, Portales and Tucumcari lie in the heart of ranching country on the high plains of the Llano Estacado of eastern New Mexico. Tucumcari, a prime tourist stop on the old US 66, still attracts travelers using nearby I-40. Clovis and Portales also are gateway cities for visitors from the Texas Panhandle and points farther east. The Santa Fe Railroad and Cannon Air Force Base are major employers in Clovis, while the economy of Portales hinges on Eastern New Mexico University and many area peanut farms.

POPULATION: Clovis, 33,400. Portales, 10,750. Tucumcari, 8,500.

ELEVATION: Clovis, 4,280 feet above sea level. Portales and Tucumcari, each 4,000 feet above sea level.

CLIMATE: July temperatures in the three communities average in the low 90s during the daytime, the mid 60s at night. In January, daytime temperatures average in the low 50s, with temperatures dipping to the low 20s at night.

PRECIPITATION: 15 inches annually in Tucumcari, 16.7 inches in Clovis and 17 inches in Portales.

SPECIAL EVENTS: In June, Pioneer Days and Balloon Fiesta in Clovis, Old Fort Days in Fort Sumner, Piñata Festival in Tucumcari; in August, Curry County Fair in Clovis, Quay County Fair in Tucumcari; in September, Roosevelt County Fair in Portales; in October, the Peanut Valley Festival in Portales.

NEARBY ATTRACTIONS: Blackwater Draw Museum, Canadian River, Caprock Amphitheatre, Fort Sumner State Monument, Grulla National Wildlife Refuge, Sumner Lake State Park and Ute Lake State Park.

Photography by Mark Nohl

Silhouette of an oil drilling rig at sunset. The oil industry, while in a slump, remains a mainstay of the Hobbs economy. This Moranco rig, working 24 hours a day, will extend down 12,500 feet.

Hobbs & Lovington

by Sharon Hendrix

D ust swirls in patterns under endless blue skies as the ribbon of highway stretches south into Lea County. Ranches spread out under fast-moving, high-flung clouds. Barbed-wire fences, laced with tawny tumbleweeds, keep you company. You're deep into New Mexico's Eastside.

Tuffy Cooper pulls his pickup into the yard at the livestock auction between Hobbs and Lovington and swings his long frame out onto the brown dirt. Lean, weathered and tan, Cooper epitomizes the spirit of the county's early settlers—individuals who literally dug in and made homes on the waterless expanse of the

Llano Estacado, the staked plains that extend into Texas.

"There's still a lot of room for individualism and ruggedness here," Cooper observes with a crooked grin. "These are family-oriented communities. There's a lot of pride and closeness that you don't see in the larger towns in the state. Most of the people are working people. They support their athletic teams. They're always here to help. . . . People who have lived in Lea County are very proud of it."

As ranchers and rodeoers, Cooper family members made their mark some years ago and also put Lea County on the map in the rodeo world. Cooper is a former National Collegiate Rodeo All-Around Champion and his son Roy and nephew Jimmy share the distinction of being National Professional Rodeo All-Around Champions.

Lea County is both ranch country and oil country. It's big, rough and raw. As large as the state of Rhode Island, the county offers many attractions, but all distinctions come from the land—wide-open stretches of shinnery oak-covered prairie that once hosted the wandering Mescalero Apaches, the Comanches and the buffalo they tracked.

Whether you enter Lea County from the west on US 380 from Roswell or US 82 from Artesia, or from due north on NM 206, a first-time visitor is struck with the breathless canopy of turquoise sky over a virtually flat and even plain. From the west and across the gently undulating Mescalero Sands, you approach the Caprock, a flat-topped wall of rock—white and chalky—stretching from north to south along the northern half of the county line. You ascend "the Cap" quickly and, once on top, you are on an expanse so level one could wonder if the ancients who thought the world was flat might be right. The land, however, actually slopes from an elevation of 4,406 feet above sea level near the Caprock off US 380 to an elevation of 2,895 at the Texas state line.

Interspersed among ranch lands and fat cattle are signposts of the oil industry that fuels the county's economy—pumpjacks nodding in the noonday sun, an occasional drilling rig piercing the cementlike caliche rock that underlies the thin layer of topsoil, crude oil storage tanks gleaming in the sun.

At the junction of NM 18 and US 82 lies the county seat, Lovington, a city of about 9,800 and one of the county's oldest settlements, outlived only by the llano's first village, Monument. Geographically, Lovington is at the center of the county. Its position as the hub of county government has long been envied by Hobbs, its bigger, gutsier neighbor to the southeast.

Located 18 miles west of Texas and 22 miles north of Hobbs, Lovington was established at the turn of the century by E. M. and J. W. Caudle, who migrated from Seminole and built the first general store. The town derived its name from R. F. Love, who in 1903 homesteaded the section that is now Lovington. The name became official when Love's brother James was appointed first postmaster. Primarily a ranching and farming center, the town became the county seat in 1917 when Lea County was formed from parts of Chavez and Eddy counties.

Hugging the Texas state line, Hobbs was a tiny ranching community until the late 1920s' discovery of oil virtually transformed it overnight into a tent city of 5,000. Hobbs boomed and busted in direct proportion to the fates of the oil and gas industry. Today it is a city of almost 30,000, the hub of the county's oil and natural gas economy.

Despite the lack of obvious tourist meccas, Lea County offers a lot to do. The open spaces, moderate temperatures and friendliness, enthusiasm and ingenuity of its people are its chief drawing cards.

With miles of blue sky and hot summer thermals to exploit, Hobbs is known around the world as a soaring mecca. Enthusiasts come from across the nation and world to sample the dry, hot, windy thermals that propel the engineless ships high into the clouds above the desert. At the height of the summer soaring season, weekend visitors are likely to see gliders' white wings etched against cerulean afternoon skies. The Hobbs Industrial Air Park, northwest of the city, is home to the Hobbs Soaring Society, the National Soaring Foundation and the Soaring Society of America. Visitors are welcome and sometimes are able to catch a ride in the summer for a nominal fee.

Boasting some of the best soaring conditions in the world, Hobbs hosted the 1983 World Soaring Championship, bringing hundreds of international glider pilots and crews to southeastern New Mexico. Now that the Soaring Society of America headquarters are in Hobbs, more events are planned each year. Regional and national contests are conducted, in addition to clinics and schools.

Within the county's boundaries, anglers enjoy Lovington's Chaparral Lake and Green Meadow Lake just north of Hobbs on NM 18, or Maddox Lake, a private fishing area west of Hobbs. Harry McAdams State Park near the Hobbs Industrial Park has overnight camping facilities.

The rolling desert offers hunters small game in season—quail, dove, prairie chicken and rabbit. Antelope can be hunted within a half-hour radius of Hobbs.

All Lea cities have top-notch sporting facilities, and Hobbs boasts lighted baseball, softball, soccer and football fields, two outdoor municipal swimming pools, an indoor pool, an 18-hole city golf course and Hobbs Country Club's manicured greens and a 13,000-seat high school stadium and track. Between 26 and 30 tournaments attract area golfers to Hobbs.

The Lea County Cowboy Hall of Fame operates a museum on the New Mexico Junior College campus, just north of Hobbs on NM 18, where memorabilia of the inductees and displays of life in the county from early man to present day can be seen. The museum also is the repository for Lea County rodeo awards, specimens of wildlife indigenous to the area and a new early man-Native American archaeological exhibit designed by Calvin Smith, a former Lea Countian and Baylor University museum curator.

The museum's six-panel needlework screen depicting the county's history is one of only two such screens in the state—the other belongs to the state of New Mexico. The panoramic screen was commissioned and stitched on 16 canvasses by volunteers and is set off by a beautiful distressed and adzed alderwood frame.

The county has several other small museums where visitors can see mementos of pioneer and ranch life. The Lea County Museum in the old Plaza Hotel in Lovington, across from the Lea County Courthouse on Love and Central streets, is home to a wealth of everyday pioneer items. Founded by the Lovington Woman's Club, it is operated by the city. The grounds house several other historic structures in various stages of restoration, including the original Love home, an old schoolhouse, a half dugout, a windmill and a sheepherder's wagon.

About five miles west of Hobbs is a small private museum founded by Lea County pioneer Thelma Webber. The rock house displays Webber's family heirlooms and artifacts and donated items from

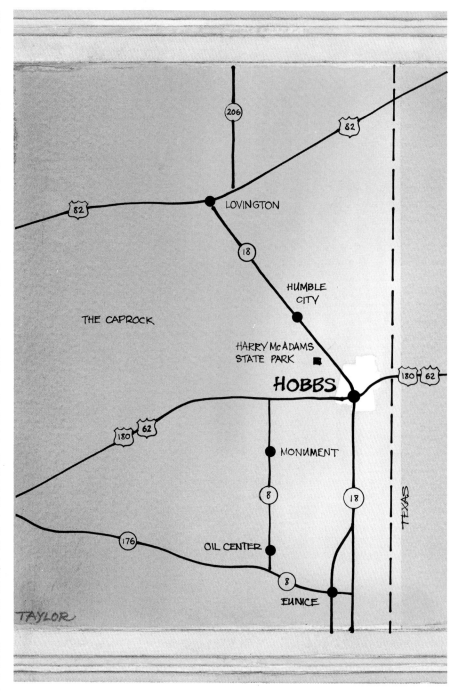

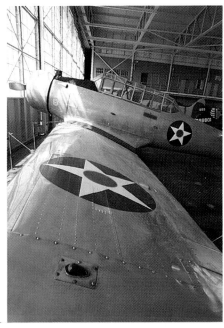

Top left—A Ryan PT22, a plane used to train pilots in the '30s and '40s, on display at the Confederate Air Force Museum. **Bottom left**—Settlers' exhibit at the Cowboy Hall of Fame.

other Lea County families. The museum is open by appointment by calling Webber at 393-4784.

The Confederate Air Force Museum, the New Mexico Wing of the Confederate Air Force, is at the Lea County Airport west of Hobbs. Open during daytime hours, visitors can see a variety of historical aircraft, including a B-25 Mitchell Bomber, two Japanese VALs, a Messerschmitt 108, a Japanese Fuji and a Beechcraft C-45. For guided tours, contact the Hobbs Chamber of Commerce.

Hobbs also is official home to the Miss New Mexico Scholarship Pageant, hosted by the Hobbs Jaycees. The pageant attracts many out-of-towners to enjoy professional entertainment and see which contestant

goes on to the Miss America Pageant.

Lea Countians are proud of their rough-and-ready heritage, and community festivals bear that identity—Hobbs' Hoedown Days and Rough 'n Ready Days, Lovington's Great Lizard Race, Eunice's Old Fiddlers' Contest and the granddaddy of them all, the yearly Lea County Fair and Rodeo.

Late summer and fall celebrations feature Western themes, beginning with the fair and rodeo in August. It's Lovington's biggest event and one the town gears up for with gusto. The fair and rodeo are among the largest in the state, both in attendance and in the number of Professional Rodeo Cowboy Association members who compete.

A parade through downtown Lovington kicks off festivities. Exhibits, a junior livestock show, a midway and other displays take place at the Lea County Fairgrounds. Events culminate with the crowning of a fair queen and professional country-Western musical entertainment.

The fairgrounds is a center for many ranch- and livestock-related events throughout the year. Playdays, horse shows and timed events are conducted there, in addition to "pickin' 'n grinnin'" jamborees each month.

September brings the annual Open Range Cowboys Association reunion, when original settlers and descendants get together to picnic and swap stories. It is followed the fourth Saturday in September by the Days of the Old West Ranch Rodeo, sponsored by the Lea County Cowboy Hall of Fame. The ranch rodeo is a day of old-time fun when members get together for authentic ranch events, such as ribbon roping, wild-cow milking and chuck wagon races.

September also brings Hobbs Hoedown Days. With a Western theme, the weekend offers a parade featuring New Mexico and West Texas sheriffs' posses, a sanctioned fiddlers' contest with cash prizes, a jail in which city notables can be incarcerated for donations to charity, a street dance, the annual chile cook-off, arts and crafts booths and displays. Merchants in Western dress greet visitors, and staged gunfights and stagecoach rides carry out the Western theme.

Also that weekend, bicyclists gather in Hobbs for the High Desert Hundred (bicycle) Stage Race, a three-event weekend sponsored by the High Plains Cyclists. The club's other big event is the May Festival Ride, scheduled in conjunction with the annual May Festival of the Arts. The ride, offering three distances for riders of varying abilities, draws hundreds of bicyclists each year.

The four-day May Festival also features a Six-State Juried Art Show, a classical music event by the New Mexico Symphony Committee at Hobbs, a two-day arts and crafts fair and a jazz-bluegrass music concert.

Windswept sandhills west of Hobbs are a playground for motorcyclists and off-road enthusiasts. Each February, the Hackberry Enduro, part of the High Plains Enduro circuit, draws about 150 riders from the region. The 75- to 90-mile race across the sandy desert is sponsored by the Caprock Rough Riders of Hobbs.

Lovington residents are proud of the city's annual Fourth of July celebration at Chaparral Park, where the highlight of the day is the World's Greatest Lizard Race. Meanwhile, at Hobbs' Fourth of July celebration, Rough 'n Ready Days, sack races, jalapeño pepper-eating contests and cow-chip tossing are the order of the day.

The holidays bring festivals to both cities. Lovington's nighttime Electric Light Parade the last weekend in November features lighted floats, cars and other conveyances that attract hundreds of out-of-town visitors. Hobbs' Holiday Heyday in early December includes a downtown parade, a two-day arts and crafts bazaar and a Christmas-tree-lighting event.

Every two years, the Hobbs and Lovington chambers of commerce cosponsor the Llano Estacado Oil and Gas Show at the fairgrounds. The show gives visitors the chance to see oilfield technology. Other area annual events are Lovington's Arts and Crafts Show in early November, the Auto Expo and antique car show in April at the fairgrounds, the annual Southeastern Home and Garden Show in May, Fiesta International in Lovington in September, Cinco de Mayo celebrations in Hobbs in May and a Mexican Rodeo in June.

Lovington's friendly small-town atmosphere welcomes visitors, who are invited to take a tour (by appointment weekdays) of La Poblanita Tortilla Factory at 400 N. East Street.

Lovington and Hobbs eateries feature hearty Western fare. Pearl's Boarding House Cafe, 318 S. Love, is known for its basic American farm fare. The Ranch House also is a longtime Lovington establishment and, according to one resident, "has been here longer than paved roads." In Hobbs, Rumors rock house restaurant is known for its Mexican food specials and excellent margaritas.

The largest city in Lea County, Hobbs is the hub of the oil and gas industry, which is responsible for 70 percent of its economy. Ranching, farming and potash mining also contribute significantly to the economy. Hobbs offers a variety of attractions for sports and outdoor enthusiasts. The desert's dry hot thermals attract soaring enthusiasts from around the world. Twenty-two miles north of Hobbs is the county seat of Lovington. In addition to government, Lovington's economy also is based on oil and gas production, farming and ranching. Lovington is home to the Lea County Fair and Rodeo, considered one of the best fairs in the state. Lea County is known for producing many professional rodeo champions.

POPULATION: Hobbs, 28,794. Lovington, 9,727.

ELEVATION: Hobbs, 3,615 feet above sea level. Lovington, 3,900 feet above sea level.

CLIMATE: July temperatures average 94 degrees in the day and 67 nights. Winters are mild and generally sunny with daytime averaging 58 degrees in January.

PRECIPITATION: Rainfall averages 10 to 15 inches per year, with moisture coming from the Gulf of Mexico. Average annual snowfall is less than 15 inches.

SPECIAL EVENTS: Lea County Fair and Rodeo in August, Hobbs Hoedown Days in September, May Festival in Hobbs, World's Greatest Lizard Race July 4 in Lovington and Rough 'n Ready Day July 4 in Hobbs.

NEARBY ATTRACTIONS: Harry McAdams State Park and Green Meadow Lake, Chaparral Lake, the Caprock and sandhills southwest of Hobbs.

The Organ Mountains, east of Las Cruces, offer a stark contrast to the plains below.

Mark Nohl

Las Cruces

by Marc Sani

When Lawrence Torres was a child growing up in Las Cruces, he would often stop and peek inside the old Amador Hotel. Now 70, he recalls those childhood moments. "It was wonderful! It was like walking into an old museum. They had figurines, santos, old Spanish beds and mockingbirds. You wouldn't believe it. They had live mockingbirds, in cages, hanging everywhere. It was really very, very colorful," says Torres.

Torres enjoys telling another story about the old Amador. In 1945, after returning home from two years in the South Pacific, Torres and his bride spent several honeymoon nights at the Amador. "Before we were married, I had to promise her father—he was the county sheriff—that we'd say the rosary every night before going to bed. When we knelt down to pray, I kicked over a floor lamp and broke it and, would you believe, they charged me for it," Torres says, laughing.

The stately Amador Hotel, where Billy the Kid and Sheriff Pat Garrett once spent their evenings, was refurbished by the Citizens Bank of Las Cruces after

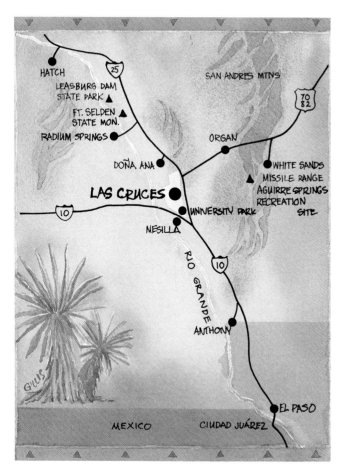

Southern New Mexico boasts many reminders of its colorful and sometimes violent past—the early development of nearby La Mesilla, the founding of Las Cruces, the written accounts of Spanish migrations northward on the Jornada del Muerto, or Journey of Death, the desolate ruins of Fort Selden built in 1865 to protect travelers from bandits and Indian attacks.

A trip to Las Cruces is quick and convenient for the weekend traveler. For example, driving from Albuquerque takes a little more than three hours on I-25. I-10 links Las Cruces, a crossroads city, with Tucson to the west and, 45 miles southeast, El Paso, Texas, and its sister city, Juárez, Mexico. I-25 ties Las Cruces to New Mexico's northern cities, while US 70 heads northeast to White Sands and Alamogordo. International ports of entry between Mexico and the U.S. are located in southern Doña Ana County at Santa Teresa and Anapra as well as at Crawford International Airport in Las Cruces.

Las Cruces is fast developing as an economic, agricultural, tourist and cultural mecca for southern New Mexico. For the winter visitor, the city offers brilliant blue skies, warm days and crisp, cool nights. "Snow birds"—those who flock to southern climes with campers and trailers—have made Las Cruces a must stop for winter travel. A tour through Las Cruces and its surrounding attractions can easily keep a visitor on the go for a few days. So where to start? A friendly and helpful staff at the Las Cruces Convention and Visitors Bureau will give you brochures and guides to all area attractions.

If you start your visit in the downtown area, use the city's National Historic Districts brochure for a self-guided tour of the Mesquite and Alameda-Depot Districts. The Mesquite District contains 159 buildings that reflect the traditional structures of old Las Cruces. Many are one-story, flat-roofed adobe homes that date from 1870. They often front on narrow streets, their simple facades stuccoed with pastel pinks, greens, blues and shades of brown.

The Alameda-Depot Historic District lies in a half-mile-wide area between the railroad tracks and the original Las Cruces townsite. The architecture, sharply contrasting with the Mesquite District, boasts a combination of adobe construction with Queen Anne, Italianate, Georgian, colonial revival and other classic styles. The Alameda area became a showplace for the latest trends in architecture. Broad lawns and extensive gardens characterize this area of the city. Other

buying it in 1969. It was recently sold to Doña Ana County. *The History of the Amador Hotel,* a brochure produced by the bank, recounts how Don Martin Amador moved his family to Las Cruces in 1850, building the Amador as a rest stop for freight-line teamsters and stagecoach passengers en route from New Orleans to San Francisco. While using the old hotel for routine business, the bank took care to preserve the rooms, antiques and memorabilia so important to the historical record of Las Cruces.

The city of Las Cruces, Spanish for "the crosses," dominates the fertile Mesilla Valley where Spanish colonizer Juan de Oñate passed through in 1598. The city was officially founded in 1849 and named in memory of 40 travelers from Taos killed by Apaches while camped in the Mesilla Valley. The city takes its name from the crosses that marked their graves.

San Albino Church in Mesilla Plaza.

significant downtown buildings include the Amador Hotel, the Doña Ana County Courthouse and the city's Branigan Cultural Center. The center boasts various collections and exhibits.

While in the downtown area, take a few moments to visit the grave of Sheriff Pat Garrett, the man who killed Billy the Kid. Garrett, while sheriff of Doña Ana County, was gunned down in an arroyo in the nearby Organ Mountains in 1908. His killer was never found. He was buried in Las Cruces' Masonic Cemetery at Brown and Compress Roads.

From downtown it is just a few minutes' drive to La Mesilla, the territorial capital of Arizona during the Confederate occupation, 1861-62. When the first territorial census was taken in 1850, La Mesilla was larger than Las Cruces; however, when the railroad bypassed it in 1880, the economic center of Doña Ana County moved from La Mesilla to Las Cruces. Patches of farmland still separate it from Las Cruces proper, but subdivisions and other developments are slowly surrounding this unique historical site.

Easily reached from I-10 via the Avenida de Mesilla exit, the plaza still retains an old-fashioned air. Visitors don't crowd the square like they do in Santa Fe, its cousin to the north. Fast-paced merchandising has yet to descend on La Mesilla. Thick-walled adobe buildings, constructed to protect the villagers from raiding Apaches, still surround the plaza. It was a major crossroads for El Camino Real and the Butterfield Overland Stage Route. The dusty old plaza was the scene of many a fight. It was a favorite watering hole for Billy the Kid and other outlaws who frequented its gambling halls and saloons. And it was here that Billy the Kid stood trial for murder, was convicted and sentenced to death. He broke out of jail before the sentence was carried out.

It was on the plaza in 1854 that U.S. troops raised the American flag, signifying annexation of La Mesilla to the United States under terms of the Gadsden Purchase, which had been signed in Mexico in 1853. The Gadsden Treaty set the boundaries between Mexico, Arizona and New Mexico that had been in dispute since the end of the Mexican War.

In 1861, La Mesilla became western headquarters for the Confederacy until it was retaken a year later by Union troops. Restaurants, galleries and nearby museums offer hours of entertainment for the visitor who wants to thoroughly explore this delightful old New Mexican village.

The Gadsden Museum at the edge of La Mesilla, along NM 28 and Barker Road, houses the collection of the Albert Jennings Fountain family, who played a significant role in the history of the area.

Nearby is the tiny village of Tortugas, home of the most southerly Indian Pueblo group in New Mexico. Located four miles south of Las Cruces off NM 478, the Tortugas live in a Hispanic village but keep their Tiwa tongue alive through their chants sung at fiesta. In early December, the Tortugas celebrate the Fiesta of Guadalupe. They perform dances and make a four-mile pilgrimage to the top of nearby A Mountain, descending by torchlight.

A good trivia question for history buffs: Where did Gen. Douglas MacArthur spend two years of his childhood? The answer: Fort Selden. Now a state monument with a new visitors center, Fort Selden was once an isolated frontier outpost where hardship was commonplace. The fort offered protection against bandits and Indian raiding parties and housed the famous Black Cavalry, or Buffalo Soldiers. It was abandoned in 1879 but reestablished two years later to house troops guarding the U.S.-Mexican border. Assigned to reactivate the post was Capt. Arthur MacArthur whose son, Douglas, would emerge as one of America's greatest and most controversial generals. Fort Selden is 10 miles north of Las Cruces. It can be reached via an exit from I-25. For those traveling south on I-25 a pleasant alternative is to take the Hatch exit and turn south on NM 85. This drive through the rich farmland bordering the Río Grande takes you past Radium Springs, a historic town built around hot mineral springs, and Leasburg Dam State Park where camping, boating and picnic facilities are open year-round.

Stahmann Farms, Inc., one of the world's largest pecan orchards, is about six miles south of La Mesilla on NM 28. Stahmann Farms, best known for its Del Cerro brand pecans, offers guided tours of its processing facilities during the winter months when pecans are readied for market. The farm tour requires a minimum party of six and about a week's advance notice. You can buy fresh pecans and candies on the farm.

Stahmann Farms was begun in 1926 when Deane Stahmann and his father bought the old Santo Tomás Farm. Only 150 acres were under cultivation, the rest were sand dunes and bosque. In 1932 the first pecan trees were planted. The average age of bearing trees today is 40, with more than 180,000 trees in production on 4,000 acres of rich farmland.

If you continue south on NM 28, which runs parallel to I-10, you will follow the traditional route used by the conquistadors on their march to northern New Mexico. The villages of La Mesilla, San Miguel, Chamberino and La Union dot the drive. Today the area is planted with cotton, alfalfa, pecans and other crops. The drive provides a backdoor approach to the cities of El Paso and Juárez and will take you to Sunland Park, where winter horse-racing enthusiasts can enjoy a day at the track.

The spectacular Organ Mountains dominate the Mesilla Valley and rise to more than 9,000 feet in elevation. The jagged peaks, dusted with snow in late winter, will draw your eye no matter where you are in the valley. Hiking trails abound in this recreational area managed by the Bureau of Land Management. To reach the mountains drive east on US 70 toward San Agustín Pass. Once through the pass, there's a pull-off and scenic overlook. A favorite spot for camping, picnics and hiking is the Aguirre Springs National Recreation Site. The entrance is about 3½ miles east of the small town of Organ off US 70. Drinking water is scarce, so take water with you.

New Mexico State University plays a major role in the community. With more than 12,000 students, the university has become a focal point for the arts in southern New Mexico. The American Southwest Theatre Company, located on campus, provides the region with first-rate theatrical performances with six shows a year. Led by Tony Award-winning playwright Mark Medoff, the theater group's influence extends throughout the Las Cruces and El Paso area.

Las Cruces also boasts a symphony orchestra sponsored by New Mexico State University and the community. The Las Cruces Symphony Association has worked to increase funding and support for the symphony and for the music department at NMSU. In 1984, the orchestra moved to the New Mexico State Music Center on campus. The building was constructed with acoustically precise walls and ceiling to enhance the orchestra's professional sound.

Las Cruces is the second most populated city in New Mexico. It offers easy access to major U.S. markets and Mexico. The fertile farmland adjacent to the Río Grande has created a cornucopia of nuts and vegetables. It is a large truck-farming area, supported by agricultural research farms at New Mexico State University. La Mesilla, a historic village, features quaint Southwestern shops. Modern Las Cruces boasts New Mexico State University, museums, art galleries and theaters. The rugged Organ Mountains are to the east.

POPULATION: Approximately 60,000.

ELEVATION: 3,896 feet above sea level.

CLIMATE: Las Cruces boasts year-round sunshine with mild winters. While summer days are warm, the evenings rapidly cool, creating a pleasant atmosphere for early evening recreation. Daytime humidity is extremely low during the summer months. The average high temperature in July is 94 degrees with a low of 65 degrees at night. The average high in January is 56 degrees with an average low of 25 degrees at night.

PRECIPITATION: Annual average is 8 inches.

SPECIAL EVENTS: Doña Ana Arts Council Renaissance Craftfaire in November, Los Pastores Christmas Play and Fiesta of Our Lady of Guadalupe in December; in the fall, the Whole Enchilada Fiesta Hot-Air Balloon Rally, Hatch Chile Festival, the Whole Enchilada Fiesta and Southern New Mexico State Fair.

NEARBY ATTRACTIONS: Aguirre Springs National Recreation Site, Sunland Park Race Track, White Sands Missile Range, Fort Selden State Monument, Leasburg Dam State Park and the town of Hatch, known for its chile fields.

El Paso/Juárez

Foreign Allure Beckons Visitors to Sister Cities

For many, a visit to Las Cruces wouldn't be complete without a side trip to El Paso, Texas, or Juárez, Mexico. A quick 45-mile drive south along I-10 puts you in the heart of El Paso in less than an hour. A leisurely drive along NM 28, which parallels the freeway, offers a more scenic route as it passes through pecan groves and irrigated cropland. For the Spanish conquistadors, El Paso was the gateway to the north, or "the Pass." Some of the oldest buildings in the United States are found in El Paso, contrasting with its downtown buildings of modern glass and concrete. El Paso is the hub for major airline transportation into the region with El Paso International Airport servicing major flights for travelers to Las Cruces.

Directly across the border is Juárez. Enjoy all the flavor of a foreign country just a short drive from downtown El Paso. The traditional shopping area in Juárez is on Juárez Avenue. The other major shopping center is the government-sponsored ProNaf. The ProNaf is filled with pottery, textiles and artworks. And for those who enjoy the bustle of a major city's marketplace, visit the City Market midway between the ProNaf and downtown Juárez. If you have never crossed the border into Mexico, fear not—no papers are needed to spend a day shopping in Juárez. Visits beyond the city, however, require a tourist card. Bring a notarized birth certificate, voter registration card or other proof of citizenship to get the permit. When returning to El Paso, be prepared to declare your purchases.

The Plaza Hotel, built in 1882, is the centerpiece of the historic restoration under way on the Old Town Plaza in Las Vegas.

Eduardo Fuss

Las Vegas

by Jean Duerlinger Bustos

L as Vegas, Spanish for "the meadows," beckons visitors to the high plains of northeastern New Mexico. The community in the shadow of the Sangre de Cristo Mountains was the state's leading center of commerce and trade in the late 19th century. That era has passed, but 900 buildings in nine historic districts still stand, as if any moment the old players will return.

Today, carefully built around old churches, saloons, shops and houses, is a town of 15,000, in the midst of New Mexico's largest architectural restoration. A local effort, the project is the work of townspeople, who

hope it will result in renovated dime stores and laundries, as well as boutiques and galleries.

To take in the area, set aside a weekend, spending Saturday night at the restored Carriage House Bed & Breakfast on Sixth Street, the historic 1882 Plaza Hotel or any of the many area accommodations. Recommendations are a stout pair of walking shoes, a tankful of gas, walking-tour brochures available at the Chamber of Commerce and the books *Gateway to Glorieta* or *Architecture and Preservation in Las Vegas*. The literature might be unnecessary for the more gregarious sightseers. Locals are proud and eager to discuss their properties.

A tour of the Plaza is a three-block hike from Bridge

Top—*The Armand Hammer World College, housed in the former Montezuma Hotel, the first building in New Mexico wired for electricity.* ***Bottom***—*Ruins at Fort Union National Monument northeast of Las Vegas.*

Street to South Pacific Street, named for trains, not islands. A Spanish colonial farm settlement, Las Vegas began here in 1835. Four sets of adobe buildings grew around the Plaza. Of these, only the old Dice Apartments survive. From that building's rooftop on August 16, 1846, newly promoted Brig. Gen. Stephen Watts Kearny proclaimed New Mexico a U.S. territory—shortly after the onset of the Mexican War.

Across the Plaza from the Dice building is the once-nefarious Imperial Bar. From about 1875 until 1884, this served as headquarters of Vicente Silva and his notorious 20-man gang. According to old-timers, Silva's ghost still haunts the Plaza because he was never buried in his own grave. It seems the impresario-turned-bandit was burying his wife, Telésfora, whom he murdered in the hills north of town, when he was slain by one of his own henchmen in April 1884.

Down Bridge Street off the Plaza's southeast corner is the old firehouse, built in 1900 for the volunteer fire department. The E. Romero Hose and Fire Company still operates, its gleaming white trucks emblazoned with the 86-year-old name. The headquarters is a more modern building a few blocks away, but the old red and white brick firehouse on Bridge Street remains. Edmundo Angel of Springer, son of a turn-of-the-century firefighter, says the early firehouse horse team was so well trained that the horses opened their own stalls when the bell clanged and assembled at the head of the wagon.

Farther east, on Sixth Street, is New Mexico's first city hall, now the police station.

Off the Plaza's southwest corner, down South Pacific Street, remains a page of old colonial Spain. Homes of original families still exist. This also was the neighborhood of another generation of old Southwest characters. Pat Garrett's house is here. Garrett—a one-time Lincoln County sheriff—is among a dozen fellows who claimed they killed Billy the Kid. He is less remembered as the father of the woman who wrote *O Fair New Mexico*, the state song.

Nearby, on Socorro Street, is New Mexico's first Protestant church, the old Presbyterian Mission. Occupied in 1872, it now is a thrift shop and occasional shelter for transients.

The visitor might reserve an evening for a glass of New Mexico wine (aged at a winery 10 miles from town) at the Castañeda, an 1898 California mission style Harvey House. Beneath the lobby's vast pressed-tin ceiling, Teddy Roosevelt, who had just returned from the San Juan Hill battle with the Rough Riders, declared his candidacy for the vice-presidency. Outside the hotel door, blackened walls and comic murals are souvenirs of a 1983 MGM movie set for *Red Dawn*.

One morning, the visitor should climb in the car, prepared for a breathtaking glimpse of nature. Heading 20 miles north on NM 65, he will climb a paved highway toward the region's landmark, Hermit's Peak. It is one of New Mexico's most spectacular drives. The road ends in the Santa Fe National Forest and in private woods. The trail up the peak stretches out among many footpaths.

Many people use guides on the arduous day's hike. Contact the

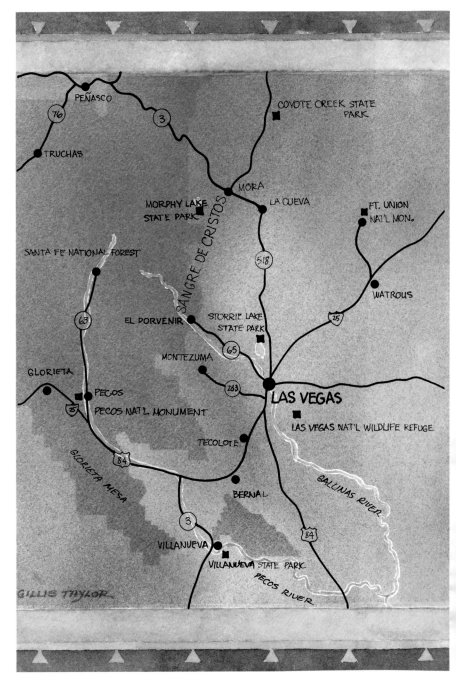

Top—A pony grazes near Puerto de Luna. The community, south of Santa Rosa, was a campsite for the Coronado Expedition in 1541. **Below**—The Rough Riders Museum in Las Vegas houses Indian artifacts, documents pertaining to the city's history and memorabilia from the Spanish-American War.

New Mexico Council on Guides and Outfitters, Box 994, Socorro, NM 87801. For the less adventurous, shady campgrounds at the foot of the mountain are flanked by a stream. Mountain jays await there, always ready for a crust of bread.

Before the hermit came, in 1863 or 1864, the red mountain was called El Cerro Tecolote, or Owl Peak. Living first in a cave near Romeroville, the hermit, Juan María Agostini, later escaped to another cave near the peak's eastern rim, living there until 1867. It was his custom, say members of the old Penitente Brotherhood of the Hermit, to light a fire each night so that those below knew he was all right. The fire reportedly was seen once in far-off La Junta, Colorado.

The hermit's firelight custom is renewed each May by members of the brotherhood, whose homes are scattered up and down the canyons. Joining them through the summer are townsfolk.

The road between Las Vegas and Hermit's Peak has four points of interest: a castle, hot spring, skating pond and scenic overlook, all in an hour's drive. First, the visitor passes the grand red brick Montezuma Castle, now part of the United World College. The center of a complex of buildings constructed between 1879 and 1890, the castle and its neighbors have served as hotels, an army hospital, a Southern Baptist college and a Mexican Jesuit seminary. Today the private campus is home to a prep school for 200 students from 60 countries.

At the foot of the grounds are public hot springs, a draw at the hotel 100 years ago and, according to legend, scene of a journey by Montezuma II, the Aztec leader who reigned from Mexico City from 1502-20. Nearby, under a cliff, is a public skating pond. During the castle's tenure as a seminary for a diocese of Mexico, the pond was a haunt of monks for prayer and for play. Farther up the road an outstanding photo opportunity exists. An overlook with a parking place abuts the road; the castle, dwarfed in the distance, sits to the east in the midst of the great softwood forest.

Also a center of Las Vegas culture is the state's turn-of-the-century teachers' college or normal school, New Mexico Highlands University. Its strong Spanish emphasis blossoms in plays by García Lorca, the music of Mexico's street bands and an abundance of Spanish poetry readings. Highlands also sponsors a Hispanic cultural festival, named the Southwest Cultural Festival. The week-long event offers workshops, readings, music and dance.

67

If these treasures are not enough, a few more pearls are still hidden.

An easy day trip from Las Vegas is to the Pecos River Valley, southwest of Las Vegas off I-25 en route to Santa Fe. Tall pine forests and the Pecos River offer a haven for camping, hiking and fishing. Villanueva State Park, amid high red sandstone bluffs, is just 31 miles southwest of Las Vegas via I-25 and NM 3.

Also in the vicinity is the Pecos National Monument. Near a river where garnets are panned, it is a sobering historic legacy—the ruins of an 800-year-old pueblo. The park is flanked by a ranch flashing the Lightning Fork brand from pink gateposts. This is the home of actress Greer Garson. In 1983 she donated 300 of the park's 340 acres and also helped pay for a $1.5 million visitor center.

Another historic attraction is the Santa Fe Trail, visible near Las Vegas 1.2 miles east of town on NM 104 and again at Fort Union National Monument, a mid-19th-century fort north on I-25.

Dedicated a national monument in 1959, Fort Union serves as a reminder of the military presence in the Southwest. The fort was built originally for two companies of Illinois volunteers. The army post also served as a hospital and a center for dry goods and cattle trade.

Poetically, the region's most picturesque ruin is untouched by improvement. At the crossroads of NM 518 and NM 442, La Cueva Mill, named for a cave, deteriorates in splendor on the bank of a little canal.

Other places worth a look are the Rough Riders city museum, a handful of art galleries specializing in Spanish colonial folk art and, 40 miles southeast of Las Vegas, the town of Santa Rosa.

Built around artesian springs, Santa Rosa offers some of New Mexico's best truck-stop cooking, situated as it is on I-40, one of the state's busiest thoroughfares. Nicknamed the City of Natural Lakes, the community is home to a cluster of public and private lakes that provide opportunities for fishing and water sports. The best-known lake is the mysterious Blue Hole, a scuba diving rite of passage.

Santa Rosa was named for a small chapel built by an early settler, Don Celso Baca, in 1879. Remains of the chapel, dedicated to St. Rose of Lima, still stand. Remains of the original Baca hacienda also may be seen.

Natural wonders in this high plains country include Gallinas Canyon, which forms the route to Hermit's Peak; Storrie Lake, popular with windsurfers; McAllister Lake, site of a national wildlife refuge, and Morphy Lake, a frequently inaccessible but nearly unspoiled state park.

Las Vegas, the seat of San Miguel County, lies where the Sangre de Cristo Mountains meet the high plains of northeastern New Mexico. Las Vegas has a rich, colorful history. The community takes great pride in its past, as evident in the extensive architectural preservation work undertaken in Las Vegas' nine national historic districts.

POPULATION: About 15,000.

ELEVATION: 6,470 feet above sea level.

CLIMATE: In summer, the nights are in the mid 50s and the days range in the mid 80s. Winter temperatures average near 20 at night and in the mid 40s during the day.

PRECIPITATION: 15.1 inches annually.

SPECIAL EVENTS: United World College International Day in April, Storrie Lake windsurfing regatta in May, Santa Rosa Days on Memorial Day weekend, Las Vegas Fiesta in July and Rough Riders Reunion in mid August.

NEARBY ATTRACTIONS: Storrie Lake State Park, Las Vegas National Wildlife Refuge, Villanueva State Park, Fort Union National Monument, Armand Hammer's United World College and, in the Santa Rosa vicinity, Blue Hole and Santa Rosa Lake State Park.

A candlelight procession marks the opening of Española's Fiesta de Juan de Oñate.

Los Alamos & Española

by Jon Bowman

Ruin your weekend. That's the catchy motto of an ambitious publicity campaign launched by the city of Los Alamos to attract tourists to the once-closed scientific enclave.

Los Alamos carved its niche in history as the birth-place of the atomic bomb. Now the city is capitalizing on prehistoric times, promoting the estimated 7,000 archaeological sites found in the vicinity, many of

Photography by Mark Nohl

Above from the left—The queen's court for Española's Oñate Fiesta, traditional fiesta wear, a scenic view looking toward the Sangre de Cristos from Los Alamos.

them concentrated at Bandelier National Monument.

Nearby Española also has discovered its past and, in the process, found a way to lure visitors to a region steeped in history and culture. In 1598, Juan de Oñate established the first European colony in the interior of this country at a cottonwood-canopied site along the Río Grande just north of Española. The Española area remains the cradle of Hispanic culture in northern New Mexico, renowned for its traditional arts and crafts, spicy regional cuisine and historic churches.

Completing the multicultural mosaic, Española lies within 25 miles of seven Indian pueblos. Without pressing too hard, it's possible in the span of a day to see María Martínez pots at San Ildefonso, tour the Puyé Cliff dwellings at Santa Clara, picnic by Nambé Falls and buy a rainbow-colored corn necklace at the O'ke Oweenge Crafts Cooperative at San Juan. Those who really hustle could stop along the way at Tesuque, Pojoaque and Picurís pueblos.

Los Alamos and Española are within an hour's drive of either Santa Fe or Taos. Few excursions can compare for scenery, especially in the fall. That's when the cottonwoods turn a plush shade of gold and the aspens in higher elevations break out into brilliant royal hues. Contributing to this colorful backdrop are the

flaming red *ristras*—strands made of chile pods—that adorn fruit stands throughout the Española Valley. Sights such as these no doubt influenced the vivid paintings of Georgia O'Keeffe, who lived in the red-rock country of Abiquiú north of Española.

O'Keeffe remains the area's most celebrated artist, but she was hardly the first. Decades before her arrival, María Martínez began to create the exquisite black pots still made by artisans at San Ildefonso and Santa Clara pueblos. A century or so earlier, artists such as Molleno and Fray Andrés Garcia carved and painted the ornate, awe-inspiring altars that continue to grace churches in Chimayó and Santa Cruz. And as early as 1692, the first Ortegas migrated from Spain to establish a tradition of fine weaving much practiced today in Chimayó.

Española is the best base from which to explore the Hispanic villages and Indian pueblos of north-central New Mexico. The city offers several choice restaurants and maintains a museum, the Bond House, that contains history exhibits and rotating art shows featuring local work. A drive is under way to create a 13-acre plaza in the museum vicinity that would be ringed by arts and crafts shops.

Before venturing from Española, take time to wan-

Above from the left—*A young dancer during Feast Day at San Juan Pueblo, whitewater rafting on the Río Grande.*

der through the many neighborhoods that have gradually been annexed to the city. Outsiders may think of Española as a distinct entity, but residents proudly declare they're from San Pedro, Hernandez, Sombrillo, Ranchitos, Fairview and more exotic-sounding bergs such as Guachupangue, Cuarteles and El Guique.

After dinner, set aside at least an hour to cruise US 285, the main north-south drag through town. It's a hotbed of action at night as automobile enthusiasts in souped-up cars called lowriders parade up and down the street. They go slow, allowing plenty of time for others to admire the hydraulic lifts, painted bodies and custom interiors that distinguish their vehicles.

Heading east from Española on NM 76, stop by Santa Cruz, the second oldest European settlement in New Mexico and site of Holy Cross Church. Its thick adobe walls have weathered the elements since 1733. Chimayó, with its famed *santuario*, lies a few more miles down NM 76 toward the Sangre de Cristo Mountains. If you drive at sunset, you can see the reddish glow of the mountains and understand why they were named "the blood of Christ."

Even though it's a small village, Chimayó can keep the visitor occupied a full day. Weavers work on hand-looms to create bright, intricately patterned Chimayó blankets at Ortega's and Trujillo's weaving shops. They also fabricate rugs, vests, ties and even seat covers. Roy Rogers and Burl Ives can be counted among the celebrities who prize this work, done in a style handed down from generation to generation.

The Santuario de Chimayó, a church built from 1814-16, has come to be known as the Lourdes of America. Crutches on the walls attest to the faith of the thousands who make pilgrimages to the church, particularly on Good Friday. Many take clay from a hole carved out of the floor because of its reputed healing powers.

No visit to Chimayó would be complete without sampling the food at Rancho de Chimayó, described by travel writer Robert L. Casey as "the best Mexican-style food in America today—bar none!" The restaurant is housed in a cozy hacienda with an extensive, terraced patio. Another Chimayó landmark is the Plaza del Cerro, an example of a fortified plaza enclosed by adobe buildings, once used as a defense against Indian raids.

Further east of Chimayó lie the villages of Córdova, known for its woodcarvers, and Truchas, where Robert Redford shot the movie *The Milagro Beanfield War*. To reach Nambé Pueblo, take NM 520 south of

Chimayó. Fishing and picnicking are popular at the Nambé Falls recreation area.

Just as many attractions await the visitor who travels north from Española. At San Juan Pueblo, five miles to the north off US 285, take in O'ke Oweenge, featuring arts and crafts by 75 tribal members. Specialties range from woven rain sashes and ceremonial ribbon shirts to pottery and corn, squash and watermelon seed necklaces.

Stay on US 285 to reach Ojo Caliente, site of mineral baths enjoyed by Indians, Spanish colonists and such latecomers as Billy the Kid and Kit Carson. Or veer off to NM 68, which passes through Velarde, Embudo and Dixon, with their apple, apricot and cherry orchards. Grape vineyards also may be seen in Dixon, home of La Chiripada winery. Many artists and craftsmen live in the community, opening their studios for a weekend tour in early November.

NM 30 and NM 502 connect Española with Los Alamos to the west. Santa Clara and San Ildefonso pueblos occupy the fertile river valley in between, shadowed by an outcropping of basalt known as Black Mesa, sacred to the pueblos.

Of all the pueblos, Santa Clara, off NM 30, offers the most organized tours for visitors. Guides not only will show off the ruins at Puyé but also take visitors on raft trips down the Río Grande, walks through the pueblo and tours of artists' studios. By advance arrangement through the pueblo or area travel agencies, you can partake of a traditional Indian feast.

Recreational opportunities abound at Santa Clara Canyon, a forested, eight-mile-long preserve with four trout lakes, a beaver dam, stream, picnic sites and developed campgrounds.

San Ildefonso Pueblo, off NM 502, also stocks a man-made trout lake and operates its own museum,

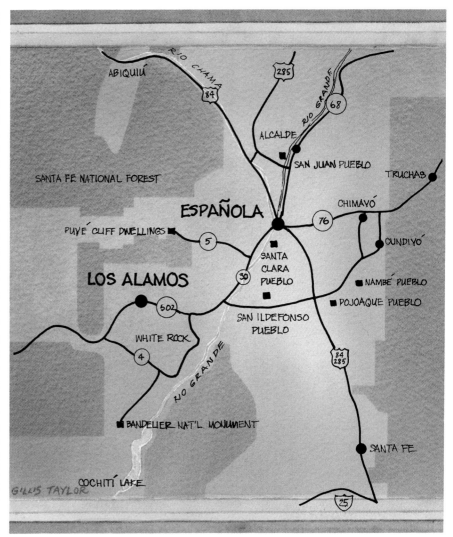

housing works by the late María Martínez, Blue Corn and other noted potters. The museum is on the outskirts of the San Ildefonso Plaza, one of the largest anywhere. Because of its size and impressive kivas, the plaza hosts the annual Eight Northern Pueblos Arts and Crafts Fair each July.

Leaving San Ildefonso behind, head west on NM 502 to Los Alamos. The journey involves a 1,700-foot climb to the top of a plateau looming 7,300 feet above sea level. The pink and white cliffs en route are formed from tuff, a volcanic rock punched with so many holes that it resembles Swiss cheese.

Feast Day at San Ildefonso Pueblo. It was the last pueblo to fall to the Spanish in the reconquest after the Pueblo Revolt of 1680. The San Ildefonso people withstood siege for four years from the top of Black Mesa.

It was this porous rock that appealed to the Indians who migrated to nearby Bandelier National Monument some 700 years ago. The cave dwellings at Bandelier serve as proof of how easy it was to carve a home out of a mountain, but life was not easy for these ancestors of the present-day San Ildefonso. The monument contains thousands of archaeological sites, mostly abandoned before the Spanish arrived.

The largest excavated sites, including kivas and condominium-style apartments, are within easy walking distance inside the stream-fed, shaded confines of Frijoles Canyon. Avid hikers can seek out more remote

sites, such as the Painted Cave and Shrine of the Stone Lions, by following the 75 miles of maintained trails in Bandelier's backcountry wilderness.

A fire in 1977 has left portions of the wilderness still scarred, but the blaze has brought benefits. Herds of elk and deer have grown fat on the ground foliage that sprung up in place of charred trees.

Los Alamos, with its glistening research facilities, stands in marked contrast to the ancient wonders of Bandelier. Most of the city's weapons and energy labs remain off-limits to the public. But the Bradbury Science Museum provides a glimpse of the work carried out for the federal government by Los Alamos National Laboratory. It's a hands-on museum, where you can align a laser, communicate with computers and detonate a simulated underground nuclear explosion.

One lab site open for tours is the Clinton P. Anderson Meson Physics Facility, a half-mile-long linear accelerator used for biomedical and advanced physics studies. Call 667-7396 to make arrangements. You also can pick up discarded scientific equipment—for instance, nose cones that will serve as ash trays—at a salvage yard, open sporadically.

In the town proper, visit Fuller Lodge, onetime headquarters of the Los Alamos Ranch School for boys, which was shut down with the creation of the lab in World War II. The stone and log lodge now houses an active arts center showing regional work, the chamber of commerce and a historical museum full of memorabilia from the boys' school era and war years. A well-manicured rose garden is kept on the grounds. There's also an authentic homesteaders' cabin.

Ask the volunteers at the historical museum for a pamphlet outlining a walking tour for downtown Los Alamos. It will lead you to Bathtub Row, the neighborhood where Robert Oppenheimer, Niels Bohr, Enrico Fermi, Hans Bethe and other scientific giants once lived. Another key stop: a monument designating the location of the Ice House, where the first atomic bomb was assembled.

If science is king in Los Alamos, recreation ranks as the crown prince. The city has an 18-hole golf course, several maintained hiking trails, a ski area, an ice skating rink, a rodeo grounds and a new indoor Olympic-sized pool. The Tour de Los Alamos, which takes place the Fourth of July weekend, is one of New Mexico's premier bike races.

Fishing, hunting, bird-watching, mountain bike riding and cross-country skiing keep visitors busy in the Jémez Mountains flanking Los Alamos on the west. Lucky hikers can stumble onto one of the many natural hot springs in the mountains.

Fortunately, you can't miss the Valle Grande. This stunning formation, a grassy mountain valley 16 miles in diameter, is all that's left of the volcano that spewed out the Bandelier tuff. In fact, the volcano sent ashes as far as Kansas in an explosion 600 times more powerful than the Mount St. Helens eruption.

The Española and Los Alamos region is a land of striking contrasts, where river valleys nestle in the shadow of two mountain ranges, where farmers live next door to nuclear scientists, where Hispanics, Indians and Anglos coexist in relative peace. From the pink and white cliffs of Los Alamos to the red-rock canyons near Abiquiú to the cottonwood groves along the Río Grande, it's a land of sweeping vistas. Lakes, streams, national forests and a ski mountain make the area a haven for recreation. It's also home to many artists, working in traditional and contemporary styles.

POPULATION: Española, about 12,000. Los Alamos, 20,000.

ELEVATION: Española, 5,585 feet above sea level. Los Alamos, 7,300 feet above sea level.

CLIMATE: Española has a moderate climate, with daytime temperatures averaging 45 in January and 90 in July. Because of its mountain setting, Los Alamos is cooler, with daytime temperatures averaging 40 in January and 80 in July.

PRECIPITATION: 9.5 inches annually in Española, about twice that in Los Alamos, including heavy snowfall in winter.

SPECIAL EVENTS: Arts and crafts fairs and tours in November in Los Alamos and Dixon, San Ildefonso Pueblo Feast Day January 23, pilgrimage to Chimayó on Good Friday, the Española Valley Rodeo on Memorial Day weekend, San Juan Pueblo Feast Day June 24, the Tour de Los Alamos bike race, the Eight Northern Pueblos Arts and Crafts Fair and Española's Oñate Festival in July, the Los Alamos County Fair in August, Santa Clara Feast Day August 12 and Española's Tricultural Arts Festival in September.

NEARBY ATTRACTIONS: Bandelier National Monument, the Valle Grande, Jémez Mountains, Santa Clara Canyon, Puyé Ruins, Black Mesa, Holy Cross Church, the Santuario de Chimayó, Santa Cruz Reservoir, Abiquiú Lake, the Río Chama and Río Grande.

Cliff ruins at Bandelier National Monument.

The lobby inside Cimarron's historic St. James Hotel. Santa Fe artist Harry Miller did the wall paintings of Don Diego de Vargas and Father Junípero Serra, who founded a mission at the current site of San Diego, California. Miller painted the works in the 1930s, when the St. James was called the Don Diego.

Ratón & Cimarron

by Jon Bowman

W hat's the most publicized tourist destination in New Mexico?

If you answered Santa Fe, Taos or Ruidoso, award yourself a silver star. But step up and claim a gold star if you chose Cimarron or the neighboring city of Ratón.

How can that be? you ask. Simple. Santa Fe, Taos and Ruidoso spend small fortunes trying to lure vacationers. In the case of Cimarron and Ratón, the publicity comes gratis. That's because these two cities, shown as part of Colfax County on road maps, are in fact the crown jewels of Marlboro Country.

Through the cigarette advertisements, photographed on the CS Cattle Company ranch near Cimarron, this region has come to symbolize a utopic West of hard-working cowboys, ornery steers and rugged, wide-open spaces. Here's one case where myth and reality merge. The gama-grass-covered plains and rimrocked mesas of northeastern New Mexico harbor some of the state's largest and oldest ranches. To the west loom the Sangre de Cristo Mountains, with their trout lakes and streams that remain cool year-round under a canopy of ponderosa pine.

Mike Freeman, publisher of the *Ratón Range* newspaper, says tourists might well stampede to the area if its true identity became widely known. A Tennessee

Top—*The Santa Fe Depot, one of the few remaining rail facilities in Ratón. Built in 1903, the depot is still used today by Amtrak passengers.* *Below*—*A triptych or sequence of three photographs showing the interior of Ratón's Shuler Theatre.*

Photography by Mark Nohl

transplant, he acknowledged, "When we arrived to scout out the place, shortly after dark, I had not seen the sky as bright or with as many stars since I was a kid. The air here is clean and fresh. The hills, the plains, the mesas and the mountains are breathtaking. It's a secret, a well-kept secret, and that's unfortunate."

Even so, the word is finally trickling out. In a recent issue of *USA Today*, travel expert Arthur Frommer identified Cimarron and its surroundings as one of the five top uncongested hideaways for a summer motor trip in America. He chalked up the allure to "the enchanting beauty of New Mexico's ghost towns, gorges and old mines."

A onetime stop on the Santa Fe Trail, Ratón now stands guard over the intersection of I-25 and US 87 seven miles south of the Colorado border. If Albuquerque, Amarillo and Denver were connected by a circle, Ratón would fall roughly at the center. Cimarron is less than an hour's drive away, 38 miles to the west via US 64.

History buffs can have a field day exploring this territory, but it also has much to offer the outdoor enthusiast. Year-round opportunities abound for hunting and fishing, as well as skiing in the winter and hiking old mining trails in the summer.

La Mesa Park in Ratón draws fans for quarter-horse and thoroughbred racing weekends and holidays. The season opens in May and extends through Labor Day. If fillies aren't your fancy, how about buffalo? A herd some 150-strong roams the rolling grasslands at the Philmont Boy Scout Ranch south of Cimarron. They're an unpredict-

Capulin Mountain National Monument.

able beast, so you're advised to keep your distance. But if you can't resist the urge to stroke the grizzly mane of a buffalo, check in with Buddy Morse at Cimarron's Old Mill Museum. He keeps a pet bison named Snuffy who just loves to be scratched.

Judging by the trees, lots of scratching goes on in the forests of nearby Vermejo Park, once the largest ranch in the United States. Look closely at the bark and you'll see telltale crisscrosses. Zorro didn't wander over from the vineyards of California. The disfiguring is the handiwork of elk that frequent this private hunting preserve. As many as 6,000 of the proud, statuesque creatures live on the 400,000-plus acre spread, representing more than one-fifth of New Mexico's entire elk population.

Many other kinds of big game can be observed in the region—the traditional hunting grounds of both the Utes and Apaches. North of Ratón, crafty wild turkeys hide out in Sugarite Canyon, site of New Mexico's newest state park. The imported ibex and aoudad, an exotic mountain sheep, have found a home along the Canadian River to the east.

Hunters who need practice should stop first at the National Rifle Association's Whittington Center outside Ratón. The 33,000-acre facility houses several rifle, shotgun and pistol ranges. It hosts training camps, national competitions and the annual Santa Fe Trail Rendezvous for costumed muzzleloaders (see accompanying story).

If you're looking for solitude, try hiking the back-

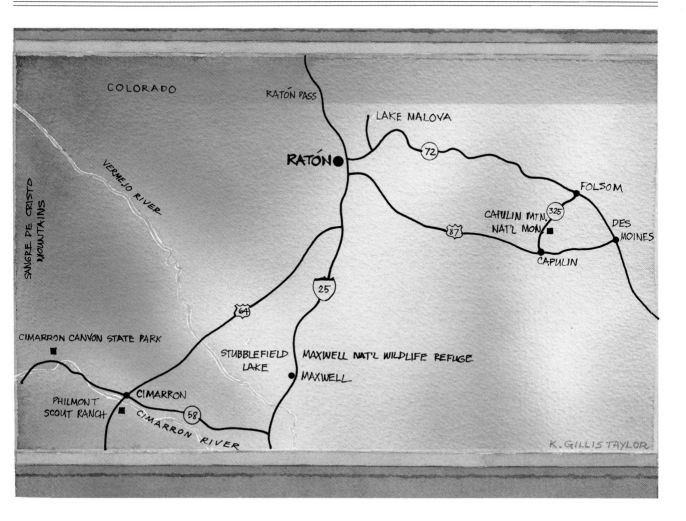

Map labels:
COLORADO
RATÓN PASS
LAKE MALOVA
RATÓN
72
FOLSOM
325
CAPULIN MTN. NAT'L MON.
DES MOINES
SANGRE DE CRISTO MOUNTAINS
VERMEJO RIVER
87
CAPULIN
25
64
CIMARRON CANYON STATE PARK
STUBBLEFIELD LAKE
MAXWELL NAT'L WILDLIFE REFUGE
MAXWELL
PHILMONT SCOUT RANCH
CIMARRON
58
CIMARRON RIVER
K. GILLIS TAYLOR

country in Valle Vidal, a portion of Vermejo Park donated to the U.S. Forest Service. Closer to civilization, try fly-fishing at Lake Maloya, the largest of three lakes inside Sugarite Canyon State Park. The trout are just as ravenous in Cimarron Creek, a pristine stream flanked by rock palisades that jut several hundred feet toward the heavens. Meanwhile, kokanee salmon challenge anglers at Eagle Nest Lake, and Springer Lake lays claim as the spawning grounds of the state's champion northern pike.

So you're not into traipsing through the woods? Then head straight for Ratón, easily spotted by the red neon Ratón sign that adorns the top of Goat Hill, visible for miles around. Former mayor Jim Wingo says Ratón offers the comforts of city life without the

headaches that usually go along with it.

"It's certainly a good place to unwind," he says. "I guess you could say the main attraction is the serenity and the ability that the area affords to do relaxing things in an unhurried way."

At an elevation of 6,666 feet, with a horseshoe-shaped shield of mesas protecting it, Ratón is spared the worst ravages of summer heat and winter cold. It's a compact city of about 9,200 people who depend on coal mining, tourism and light manufacturing for economic sustenance. The city boomed overnight after it was selected by the Atchison, Topeka and Santa Fe Railroad as the site for a repair shop in 1879. Within a year, the population hit 3,000. Unlike the tent cities that sprang up in the many mining camps in the

vicinity, the first residents of Ratón took temporary shelter in boxcars parked on sidings next to the AT&SF tracks.

No visit to Ratón would be complete without a walking tour of the downtown historic district straddling First Street, formerly known as Railroad Avenue. The Palace Hotel, now a restaurant, serves as the most opulent reminder of the days when Ratón was known as the Pittsburgh of New Mexico. With its sandstone exterior, the three-story 1896 building looks ordinary enough from the outside. But inside, elegant stained-glass fixtures, crystal chandeliers, a mahogany bar and 19th-century oil paintings tell another story.

After basking in the nostalgic atmosphere at the Palace, walk half a block to the former Coors Building, now the Ratón Museum. Let Tom Burch show you the collection of antiques, mementos, Indian artifacts and historic photographs. Much of it represents his private stock. "I'm still living in the house my grandfather built in the 1880s," he says. "They never threw anything away. It's coming in handy now."

Many other buildings in Ratón are worth a look. Stop by the Colfax County Courthouse, with its Art Deco trimmings. See the Santa Fe Depot, done in Spanish mission revival style. No matter how crowded your itinerary, make time to peek into the Shuler Theatre. It's heralded as an example of European rococo architecture, but that doesn't begin to convey the splendor of the palatial, 480-seat theater with ornate woodwork, gold-trimmed box seats and a high-topped ceiling painted to resemble the sky. Eight Manville Chapman murals, commissioned by the government during the Depression years, adorn the lobby of the Shuler. It once housed City Hall and still is a focal point for community concerts, plays and civic gatherings.

For an unusual perspective on the past, charter a plane at Crews Municipal Field. From the air, it's easy to trace the outlines of the Santa Fe Trail. Deep wagon-wheel ruts, extending 100 feet across in some cases, can be spotted along US 64 from Ratón to Cimarron.

Earthbound visitors will have a harder time keeping track of the pioneer route. But they can poke around the remains of Colfax County's many abandoned coal- and gold-mining towns. In Sugarite, for instance, look for the outline of the soccer field used by immigrant miners from Europe. Nothing is left standing at the once-formidable coal town of Dawson except a cemetery. Notice how many of the tombstones bear dates from 1913 and 1923, when tragic mining disasters occurred.

Long before Ratón was established, Cimarron made its mark in the history books, living up to its "Spanglish" name as a wild place. The town grew up around the home of Lucien Maxwell, who, in the mid-1800s, owned the largest spread in the United States—the 1.74 million-acre Maxwell Land Grant. The discovery of gold on Baldy Mountain attracted prospectors, merchants, soldiers, scarlet ladies and the West's most infamous desperadoes to Cimarron. They bought supplies at Maxwell's four-story grist mill, preserved as the Old Mill Museum. It's open weekends until Memorial Day and then daily, except Thursdays, through the summer.

Down the lane from the mill stands the pink adobe St. James Hotel, where townsfolk partied and relaxed. Built beginning in 1873 by Henri Lambert, a former cook for Gen. Ulysses S. Grant and President Abraham Lincoln, the 36-room hotel was one of the most exquisite in the West. But that didn't stop guests from shooting up the place. Of course, what can you expect when your clientele includes such colorful figures as Jesse James, Blackjack Ketchum, Wyatt Earp, Bob Ford, Pat Garrett, Doc Holliday, Buffalo Bill Cody and

Annie Oakley?

The worst of the lot, as far as the locals were concerned, was Clay Allison. Nicknamed the Gentleman Bandit, he forgot all about etiquette when he killed his 15 victims. He had another relapse the time he danced naked on top of the St. James bar.

Current St. James owners Ed and Pat Sitzberger proudly point out their new renovations such as aviaries and a pool of koi (Japanese carp) in the hotel lobby. But they're even happier to show off the authentic Victorian furnishings in rooms where outlaws were later followed by the likes of Zane Grey and Frederic Remington. For the insatiably curious, there are always the 29 bullet holes in the pressed-tin ceiling of the hotel saloon. Ed notes the ceiling originally was made of wood. "I understand it was all splinters."

Cimarron had settled down considerably by the time Oklahoma oilman Waite Phillips—of the Phillips 66 family—built his summer vacation home on a nearby ranch. The 1920s Mediterranean-style bungalow, a mansion by most standards, looks out over what is now Philmont, the Boy Scouts' wilderness retreat and adventure center. By prior arrangement, tour Villa Philmonte. It radiates wealth and class, down to the basement trophy room where Phillips entertained comedian Will Rogers and Charles Dawes, vice-president under Calvin Coolidge.

Before leaving Philmont, also be sure to browse through the Philmont Museum and Seton Memorial Library, housing the books and art of famed naturalist, author and first Chief Scout of the Boy Scouts of America Ernest Thompson Seton. Seven miles south in Rayado, the Boy Scouts have restored a hacienda once owned by Kit Carson. The building has been converted into a museum, with a working blacksmith shop.

If you're planning a summer trip, try to make it to Cimarron's Maverick Club Rodeo July 4. It's the state's oldest rodeo for working cowboys.

Another highlight of the season comes Labor Day weekend, celebrated as Cimarron Days. It's capped off by a community barbecue featuring buffalo burgers. Connoisseurs swear they taste like Sloppy Joes.

Wintertime visitors to the area have several skiing and snowmobiling options. The family-owned Sugarite Ski Basin north of Ratón offers downhill trails for beginning and intermediate skiers. From Cimarron, visitors can easily take in Sugarite as well as resorts at Sipapu, Angel Fire, Taos, Red River and Río Costilla.

Ratón, the gateway city to northeastern New Mexico, is a onetime stop on the mountain branch of the Santa Fe Trail that prospered as a center for coal mining and rail traffic. Mining remains the major industry, but tourism has grown in importance for the historic frontier community. Visitors are attracted by La Mesa Park with its horse racing, the Sugarite Ski Basin and many area lakes and parks that offer opportunities for outdoor recreation. Hunting is particularly popular in the nearby Cimarron area.

POPULATION: Ratón, about 9,200. Cimarron, about 900.

ELEVATION: Ratón, 6,666 feet above sea level. Cimarron, 6,427 feet above sea level.

CLIMATE: Surrounded by a *rincón* or horseshoe of mountains and mesas, Ratón is shielded from weather extremes. The mild, dry climate features daytime temperatures averaging 43 in January and 84 in July.

PRECIPITATION: 15.4 inches annually.

SPECIAL EVENTS: Santa Fe Trail Rendezvous in Coal Canyon in June, PRCA rodeo and parade in Ratón in June, Fourth of July celebration in Cimarron featuring week-long Western art show and annual Maverick Club Rodeo, Colfax County Fair in August, Cimarron Days celebration with dances, arts and crafts show and buffalo barbecue in September.

NEARBY ATTRACTIONS: Sugarite Canyon State Park, Elizabethtown and Colfax ghost towns, Capulin Volcano National Monument, Cimarron Canyon State Park, Philmont Scout Ranch, Valle Vidal, Cimarron Palisades, Eagle Nest and Springer lakes.

MOUNTAIN MAN RENDEZVOUS

Two mountain men relax with morning coffee after a night of hooraying.

Photos by Joe Hedrick

by Barbara Hays

The boom of black powder muskets, the smell of campfire smoke and the sight of people dressed in calico and buckskin evoke a scene out of the past. Actually, it is the Santa Fe Trail Rendezvous, where participants have fun recreating the mountain man era of the 1800s.

The rendezvous occurs in June in Coal Canyon at the National Rifle Association's Whittington Center, five miles west of Ratón on NM 555. The historic Santa Fe Trail crosses the southeast portion of the center.

This gathering attracts people who want to leave the hi-tech world behind for a long weekend of camping and activities that simulate the life of the mountain men.

Frank Salcido, a Navajo who often attends rendezvous, says many people wish they lived in earlier

Spencer Nutima, a Hopi, prepares his gun for firing.

people who enjoyed shooting muzzleloading black powder guns. It has evolved into an encampment of more than 600 people, a number that grows every year. There are two villages in the encampment separated by a stream and by participants' lifestyles.

Tepee Village is for the purist. Its inhabitants must live in old-style wall tents, lean-tos or tepees. They must dress in pre-1840 clothing, including buckskin, calico or tradecloth. Tantalizing aromas emanate from the big iron kettles suspended from tripods over open fires. Many of the tepees are gaily painted with Indian designs. Colorful ribbons flutter from the tepee poles to lend a festive air. Most activity centers around the Council Ring, located in the middle of Tepee Village.

The other village, dubbed Alcoa Village, is for those who prefer to watch other people living the primitive life. Residents of this village live in their recreational vehicles, dress as they please and can prepare TV dinners in their microwaves.

Anyone in the encampment can participate in the activities although some require period attire. The contests, with categories for all ages, include black powder shoots, hawking (ax throwing) and knife throwing. At night, there are council fires, costume and liars' contests, music, guest speakers and award presentations. A special Saturday afternoon ceremony commemorates the Santa Fe Trail and the mountain men who opened the West.

The original rendezvous were based on trade since money had no value in the wilderness. Traders active at this rendezvous will deal in skins, guns, furs, beads, knives and clothing. Don't worry if you have nothing to trade—money is always accepted.

Rendezvous were a melting pot for people of several nationalities. Many mountain men were French. They gave rendezvous its name. The headman of a rendezvous is called the "booshway," which is a corruption of the French word *bourgeois.* Next in command is the *segundo,* indicating the Spanish influence. Some people who return every year have taken Indian names.

Fees are $10 per person or $25 per family. Pets are not allowed. For more information write the Whittington Center Rendezvous, PO Box 700, Ratón, NM 87740.

times when life was simpler. "The mountain man rendezvous is an opportunity for me to recreate the fur trade era," he says. "For a few days, [I can] live and experience what life was like in the past."

The original mountain men were rugged individuals who trapped beaver from 1825 to 1840 until beaver hats went out of style. These men led solitary lives until the annual summer rendezvous. Then they came out of the mountains to trade their beaver pelts with the fur companies and Indians in exchange for food and whiskey. It was a time for swapping yarns, hooraying (partying) and making up for 11 months of loneliness.

Because romanticized exploits of that era appeal to people today, rendezvous are planned every weekend through the summer throughout the West. The Santa Fe Trail Rendezvous began in 1975 with a group of

The Chaves County Courthouse is the center of area government in Roswell.

Roswell

by Marc Sani

Locals call them Pecos Valley diamonds, small chunks of quartz found hidden in the red cliffs that thrust upward from the Pecos River six miles east of Roswell. The "diamonds" are an exciting find for scores of rock hounds who routinely visit Roswell to hunt this unique crystal found nowhere else in the United States in this form.

But there's more glitter to Roswell than just Pecos Valley diamonds. This growing economic center set in the heart of the grassy Pecos Valley of eastern New Mexico boasts a variety of attractions guaranteed to keep the weekend visitor busy. If it's rocketry that interests you, look no farther than a painstaking re-creation of Dr. Robert Goddard's workshop housed at the Roswell Museum and Art Center. Or, if military history piques your imagination, visit the Gen. Douglas L. McBride Museum at the New Mexico Military Institute.

And for those who enjoy wildlife, the renowned Bitter Lake National Wildlife Refuge is a 20-minute drive from the city. Western lore also abounds in Roswell. Here one of America's most famous cattle barons, John Chisum, headquartered his ranch—an empire that stretched 200 miles south from Fort Sumner on the Pecos River to the Texas border.

This also is Peter Hurd country. Born in Roswell in 1904, the famous artist lived 40 miles west of Roswell in the Hondo Valley near San Patricio with his artist wife, Henriette Wyeth. Some of his works, and those of his wife, hang proudly in the Roswell Museum and

*Above left—Cranes fly in formation at sundown at Bitter Lake National Wildlife Refuge. **Above right**—The New Mexico Military Institute is known as the West Point of the West.*

Art Center. And for the true Hurd aficionado, work painted while he was a World War II war correspondent for *Life Magazine* can be viewed at the McBride Museum.

Roswell, New Mexico's fourth largest city with 47,000 people, is a hub for the southeastern section of the state and sits astride a crossroad of highways. US 285 links Roswell to I-40 in the north; Artesia and Carlsbad to the south. Traffic flowing along I-25 reaches Roswell via US 380 as it cuts east at the San Antonio exit 10 miles south of Socorro. And US 70, which joins US 285 a few miles north of Roswell, ties the city to its northeastern neighbor, Clovis.

When Will Rogers, one of America's great humorists, visited Roswell in the 1930s, he called it the "prettiest little town in the West." *Money Magazine* recently called Roswell one of the nation's "Ten Towns Worth Calling Home" and then included Roswell on its list of "Peaceable Places to Retire." The city also is featured prominently in Hugh Bayless' book *The Best Towns in America.*

A weekend visit to Roswell can easily start at the Roswell Museum and Art Center. Created by the city in 1937, it's located at the corner of Main Street and 100 West 11th Street near the downtown center. A rocket launching tower stands like a beacon in front of the museum. It was built by Robert Goddard, a pioneer in American rocketry, for early rocket experiments near Roswell from 1930 to 1941. Donated to the city by his widow in 1945, the tower contains a replica of one of Goddard's early rockets. The museum houses a vast array of his tools, handmade rocket components and workbenches in its Robert A. Goddard Spacewing. In a separate display, visitors can view the original space suit—complete with dirt smudges—worn by former New Mexico senator and astronaut Harrison Schmitt when he stepped on the surface of the moon.

The museum's scope not only spans the nation's early attempts at space rocketry but also provides a vivid glimpse into the early days of the Western frontier. The Rogers Aston Collection includes more than 1,200 artifacts that trace New Mexico's Native American culture, the arrival and impact of the Spanish conquistadors, the arrival of the mountain men and the firearms and weapons used by the Plains Indians and the United States Cavalry.

The painting and sculpture collection housed permanently at the museum contains work by Georgia O'Keeffe, Andrew Dasburg, Howard Cook, Marsden Hartley, John Marin, Stuart Davis, John Sloan and Agnes Martin, plus a number of Hurd works. This collection of paintings and sculpture is based on 20th-century American art produced in the Southwest.

Roswell is proud of its historical heritage, and that pride shows in the support given to the Chaves County Historical Museum. The museum is a living history of Roswell and turn-of-the-century life in southeastern New Mexico. It is housed in an outstanding example of a prairie-style home first developed by Frank Lloyd Wright.

The house, built in 1910 with gently sweeping rooflines and large verandas for James Phelps White and his family, is a Roswell landmark. Inside, hundreds of late 19th- and early 20th-century artifacts, many donated by local residents, are on display. The kitchen is painstakingly re-created to depict a typical setting found at the turn of the century. Victorian-era furniture, stained-glass windows, exhibits of early-day telephones, fashions, phonographs, tableware and toys are well displayed throughout the home. Located at the corner of Lea and US 70/380, it is only a short drive from the Roswell Museum and Art Center.

A trip to Roswell should include a walking tour of the New Mexico Military Institute (NMMI). Located along North Main Street, this West Point of the West has graduated such well-known personalities as Peter Hurd, historian Paul Horgan, ABC newsman Sam Donaldson and others. NMMI is the only state-supported, coeducational, military junior college in the nation. On campus, visitors will marvel at the Gothic architecture that prevails throughout its buildings.

Located near the geographic center of the campus is the Gen. Douglas L. McBride Museum. This public museum, operated with the state's Office of Cultural Affairs, has displays that portray the role of New Mexico's citizens in the armed conflicts of the 20th century and the Spanish-American War. A rotating series

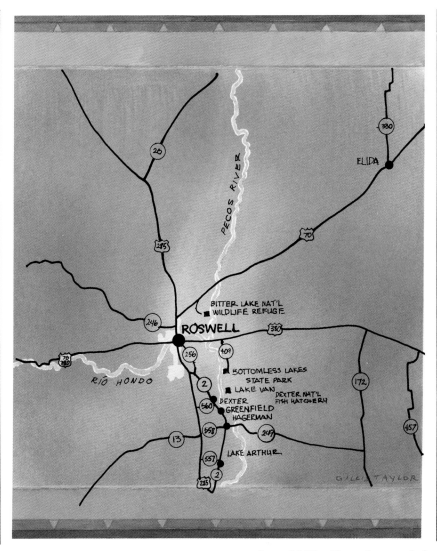

of graphic paintings of World War II combat made by American artists, such as those by Peter Hurd for *Life Magazine*, are on display. The paintings were made on the battlefronts of Europe, Africa and the South Pacific.

Continuing through Roswell, leave the NMMI campus and drive north along Main Street (US 285), heading out of the city toward the Bitter Lake National Wildlife Refuge. At Roswell's largest shopping center, a well-placed sign indicates a right turn onto the old Roswell-Clovis highway. A 20-minute drive through the rolling countryside leads directly to the Bitter Lake refuge along the Pecos River.

The refuge is a focal point for thousands of waterfowl that migrate to the area during winter. Established in 1937, the refuge centers on a small alkaline lake fed by intermittent streams and six man-made ponds, creating more than 750 acres of water surface. The refuge itself, however, totals more than 23,300 acres of brushy sand dunes, grasslands and alkali flats. Refuge headquarters is located 11 miles northeast of Roswell and is the entrance for a loop road that traverses the wildlife area. Self-guiding leaflets for a car trip through the refuge are available at the entrance. Picnic tables provide a place for a lunchtime stop along the loop. More than 280 bird species have been recorded at the refuge, and visitors can also sometimes spot mule deer, cottontails, jackrabbits and raccoons.

Another popular area near Roswell is Bottomless Lakes State Park —New Mexico's first state park, dedicated in 1933. Bottomless Lakes, a unique geographic area, is a quick 12-mile drive east of Roswell along US 70/380. Turn right onto NM 409, a short road that drops down from the bluffs overlooking the Pecos River and loops around the lakes, returning to the main highway. The lakes are not really lakes but a series of eight sinkholes, with names such as Devil's Inkwell, Lazy Lagoon, Figure Eight Lake and Mirror Lake. The park's visitor center is at Cottonwood Lake near the center of the park. The lakes were a historic stopover point for cowboys herding cattle through the New Mexico Territory. They called them Bottomless Lakes after trying to plumb the depths with their lariats with no success. Tales of underwater monsters and secret underground caves stretching to Carlsbad have added spice to local legend, but authorities say none of them are true.

Visitors touring the Roswell area should check with the chamber of commerce for the latest schedule of events produced by the Roswell Community Little Theatre, the Roswell Symphony Orchestra and the Roswell Community Concert Association.

Top and bottom—A variety of interesting exhibits are on display at the Roswell Museum and Art Center and at the Gen. Douglas L. McBride Museum.

Roswell has a diversified economy based on irrigated farming, livestock, dairy production, oil, tourism and education. Visitors can view magnificent wildlife at Bitter Lake National Wildlife Refuge or travel west through Roswell to the mountain community of Ruidoso. Roswell is approximately 200 miles southeast of Albuquerque and 206 miles northeast of El Paso, Texas.

POPULATION: Approximately 47,000.

ELEVATION: 3,570 feet above sea level.

TERRAIN: Western plains with cool alpine mountains 70 miles to the west.

CLIMATE: Roswell enjoys year-round sunshine in a semiarid climate with low humidity. Winters are mild with average mean temperatures in the mid-40s; warm summers average in the 80s.

PRECIPITATION: Annual average is 9.6 inches.

SPECIAL EVENTS: Roswell hosts its Dairy Day celebration in June with the Lake Van Milk Carton race highlighting the event. Roswell hosts the Eastern New Mexico State Fair every fall.

Lake Mescalero at the Inn of the Mountain Gods, just a canyon away from downtown Ruidoso.

Herb Brunell

Ruidoso

by Jon Bowman

Entering Ruidoso, a billboard proclaims "The Year-Around Playground of the Southwest." The slogan fits. And someone must have been thinking when they placed the billboard along US 380 extending eastward to Texas.

Ruidoso, the premiere resort town in southern New Mexico, attracts as many as 30,000 visitors on prime weekends. More than half come from Texas, seeking snow in the winter and relief from the sweltering Lone Star sun in the summer months.

Not all the signs in Ruidoso point to Texas. What makes the community special is its combination of New Mexican charm, Texan-flavored hospitality and some of the most picturesque scenery this side of the Pecos. Where else can you sample a Terlingua-style chile cook-off and cool off with fresh cherry cider from the Hondo Valley before taking in a horse race or traversing a pristine trout stream?

Ruidoso started as a ranching and lumbering center but quickly emerged as a mountain hideaway—a cool, heavily forested oasis in an otherwise arid region. Those who could afford it built summer cabins—rustic cedar castles that still stand shrouded under the thick pine cover of Ruidoso's Upper Canyon district. The less affluent enjoyed weekend flings in one of New Mexico's most wide-open towns.

As late as World War II, casino-style gambling flourished in Ruidoso. State authorities eventually seized the slot machines, but Ruidoso found another outlet for high stakes entertainment in its race track. Today, Ruidoso Downs mounts the world's richest quarter-horse race, the All-American Futurity with a multimillion dollar purse.

No matter where you're coming from, the drive into Ruidoso is uplifting. From El Paso, 124 miles to the south, follow US 54 to Tularosa, then veer east on US 70 through the 460,000-acre Mescalero Apache Reservation, home of the world-class Inn of the Mountain Gods resort. Ruidoso lies just north of the reservation boundaries in the shadow of Sierra Blanca or Old Baldy, which at 12,003 feet, looms as the highest mountain so far south in the United States.

To reach Ruidoso from Roswell, travel US 380 west about 80 miles. The route crosses through scenic Hondo Valley, home of some of New Mexico's most productive fruit orchards. Artists such as Peter Hurd and Henriette Wyeth have immortalized the rolling hills and rugged ranchers they found along the Río Hondo.

From Albuquerque, take I-25 south and swing east on US 380. Be sure to stop along the way at Valley of Fires State Park, a gnarled, black lava flow that stretches west of Carrizozo, contrasting sharply with the gypsum dunes at White Sands National Monument a few miles farther south.

In winter, Sierra Blanca beckons visitors to Ruidoso. The mountain provides a panoramic backdrop for the Ski Apache resort, formerly called Sierra Blanca. Thirty-five trails extend down the slopes, which collect as much as 360 inches of snow in a season.

Ski Apache—owned by the Mescaleros—typically opens by Thanksgiving, with skiing continuing through mid-April. There's a mix of runs for beginning and expert skiers. Skiers and sightseers can reach the summit in one of several lifts, including the state's only gondola.

Visitors can expect temperatures a good 10 to 15 degrees warmer than those at resorts in northern New Mexico and Colorado. At Ski Apache, skiers can feel the thrill of cruising down fine white powder while looking out over the White Sands below.

Steep terrain in the Ruidoso vicinity limits opportunities for other winter sports, but cross-country skiing, sledding parties and snowmobile tours can be arranged in nearby Cloudcroft.

The Chamber of Commerce and another merchants' group, the Spirit of Ruidoso, sponsor spring festivals, fairs and jamborees to fill the gap between the skiing and horse-racing seasons.

Champion thoroughbreds and quarter horses strut their stuff at the Ruidoso Downs track. Racing begins mid-May and culminates Labor Day with the All-American Futurity.

In 1986, Ruidoso Downs became the first track in the United States to install separate racing surfaces for thoroughbreds and quarter horses. More than $6 million was spent on a seven-furlong thoroughbred course. To introduce the course, the Downs unveiled a new race, the Kachina Stakes, which joins a long list of annual derbies with large, guaranteed purses—three in excess of $1 million.

Those who would rather ride horses than watch them can rent trusty steeds at private stables. Riding trails crisscross much of the Lincoln National Forest to the north and west of Ruidoso, including the White Mountain and Capitán wilderness areas. The entire forest is a hiker's paradise. Bountiful wildflowers provide ample foliage for elk, deer, mountain lions, bears and wild turkeys.

Fall is hunting season, but cold water fishing extends all year long, except at Bonito Lake, which closes through the winter. Trout is king at Nogal and Alto lakes and in the Sacramento Mountain streams for which Ruidoso is renowned. After all, this city of 9,000 is named for the "noisy" river, the Río Ruidoso, that runs parallel to Sudderth Drive in the heart of the Midtown shopping district.

Here you'll find many of Ruidoso's art galleries, boutiques, antique shops and restaurants, ranging from steakhouses to gourmet establishments. New shopping centers, including Ruidoso's first enclosed mall and a multistory financial complex, have been built along Mechem Drive, extending north from Sudderth.

Visitors can unwind at nightclubs featuring live country and rock bands. They also can take advantage of the city's many tennis courts and two championship 18-hole golf courses. Accommodations range from A-frames, log cabins and condominiums to the Inn of the Mountain Gods, with its own golf course and luxury suites overlooking Lake Mescalero.

Given all the new construction, it would seem Ruidoso risks becoming too congested. Not so. Canyons cutting through the city prohibit extensive tract

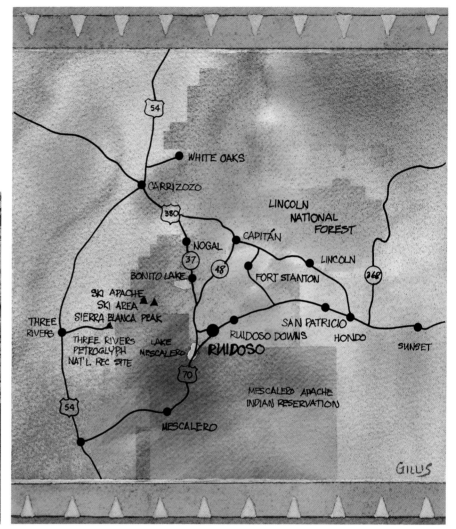

Map labels:

54
WHITE OAKS
CARRIZOZO
LINCOLN NATIONAL FOREST
380
NOGAL
37
CAPITÁN
LINCOLN
48
BONITO LAKE
FORT STANTON
368
SKI APACHE SKI AREA
SIERRA BLANCA PEAK
THREE RIVERS
RUIDOSO DOWNS
SAN PATRICIO
THREE RIVERS PETROGLYPH NAT'L REC SITE
LAKE MESCALERO
RUIDOSO
HONDO
SUNSET
70
MESCALERO APACHE INDIAN RESERVATION
54
MESCALERO
GILLIS

Above—*Autumn scene atop the Capitán Mountains north of Ruidoso.* ***Right***—*The lodge at Ski Apache.*

development. Besides, residents take pride in allowing as many trees as possible to stand, even ones that jut through garages and decks. Here's one community where it makes perfect sense to name the cemetery Forest Lawn.

If you want to avoid the crush of the crowd, fall is probably the best time to plan a Ruidoso getaway. Scheduled activities include mule races at the Downs and a motorcycle rally in September. October brings an Aspenfest parade, bicycle hill climb and Wurstfest. Aspen viewing reaches its peak the same month, as groves throughout the forest turn brilliant shades of red, yellow and gold.

As a relatively new city, Ruidoso has few historic buildings. But you need not travel far to relive the colorful days when Billy the Kid, John Chisum and others of their ilk engaged in the bloody Lincoln County range war. The violence, which riveted the nation, erupted in 1878 in the town of Lincoln to the northeast of Ruidoso on US 380. The state has preserved Lincoln as a historic district administered by the Museum of New Mexico (see accompanying story).

Eight miles west of Lincoln, history of a more recent vintage is enshrined at Smokey Bear Historical State Park in Capitán. Smokey, the bear cub rescued from a forest fire, became a national symbol for fire prevention efforts. He's buried under a boulder in the park, surrounded by native Southwest plants. Before heading down the road, check out the Smokey Bear Museum, built by Capitán volunteers. The museum has the world's largest collection of Smokey memorabilia, from windup dolls and comic books to silver medallions.

Below—Ruidoso Downs.

Mark Nohl

With a downhill ski area 16 miles away and a horse track nearby, the mountain city of Ruidoso stands as southern New Mexico's leading resort spot. The economy is fueled by tourism, the arts and recreation. Ruidoso also has a growing community of retirees, attracted by the mild climate and breathtaking scenery.

POPULATION: About 9,000, but the figure fluctuates dramatically depending on the season.

ELEVATION: 6,911 feet above sea level.

CLIMATE: Temperatures average 41 degrees in January and 60 degrees in July. Nights are crisp throughout the year.

PRECIPITATION: Annual average is 23.5 inches.

SPECIAL EVENTS: Lincoln County Art Show in May, Texas Appreciation Day in June, Coming of Age rites, Indian dances and rodeo at Mescalero in July, Smokey Bear Stampede and parade at Capitán in July, art festival in July, Billy the Kid Pageant at Lincoln in August, Lincoln County Fair at Capitán in August, Golden Aspen Motorcycle Rally in September, open championship chile cook-off in October, Southern Rockies Alpine Wurstfest with German food and dancing in October.

NEARBY ATTRACTIONS: Ski Apache resort, Ruidoso Downs race track, Mescalero Apache Indian Reservation, White Oaks ghost town, Lincoln State Monument, Valley of Fires State Park, Bonito Lake, Smokey Bear Museum and Historical State Park.

LINCOLN

Mark Nohl

The old Lincoln County Courthouse.

Wild West Heritage Preserved at Lincoln

Look closely at the bulky wooden doors of the Tunstall Store in Lincoln and you'll notice a metal shield embedded inside. The partition has stood more than a century, long before energy conservation became a concern. Merchant John Tunstall had the special doors installed for protection of another kind. His Regulators, including Billy the Kid, dodged stray bullets as they fought the bloody Lincoln County range war in the late 1870s.

Lincoln, northeast of Ruidoso along US 380, stands as testament to a violent era in American history. The Museum of New Mexico and Lincoln County Heritage Trust have acquired most of the town and restored the buildings so they look much like they did when The Kid, Pat Garrett, John Chisum and other legendary Wild West figures locked horns.

Gary Miller, curator for the Heritage Trust, says Lincoln has emerged as the Williamsburg of the West. With the town's landmark buildings now largely preserved, he hopes to give visitors more of a flavor of frontier life.

"The last 10 years have been spent on nuts and bolts, mortar and bricks," Miller says. "Now, we're trying to get involved in an educational program. We'd like to have some people dress in period costumes, do more living history. Of course, it takes money and personnel."

Besides the Tunstall Store with its period museum, Lincoln attractions include a circular rock tower called the Torreón where settlers hid during Indian raids and the old Lincoln County Courthouse, site of a dramatic jail break by Billy the Kid. Victorian furnishings give a nostalgic air to the guest rooms and dining hall at the reconstructed Wortley Hotel, once owned by Pat Garrett.

For information on Lincoln, contact the Museum of New Mexico, Monuments Bureau, PO Box 2087, Santa Fe, NM 87504 (telephone 827-8940) or the Lincoln County Heritage Trust, Lincoln, New Mexico 88338 (telephone 653-4372).

—**Jon Bowman**

Snow blankets Cathedral Park and St. Francis Cathedral in downtown Santa Fe.

Mark Nohl

Santa Fe

by Emily Drabanski

A few years ago, the Santa Fe Chamber of Commerce promoted the slogan, "I'm high on Santa Fe." In wintertime, there is something absolutely intoxicating about inhaling the heady scent of burning piñon smoke wafting in the high-altitude air. Add to that the exhilaration of breaking the morning silence as you crunch through snow covering the Plaza to reach your favorite cafe for a steaming bowl of chile and fresh tortillas—it's hard to beat. Skiers, in particular, will find that the Santa Fe Ski Area offers the ulti-

mate high in Santa Fe.

Even Scrooge would have a hard time bah-humbugging the holiday spirit that permeates Santa Fe during December. *Feliz Navidad* is the traditional Spanish Christmas greeting. In Santa Fe, it means streets lined with *farolitos* (candles in sand-filled paper bags) and *luminarias* (bonfires) that families and friends warm themselves by on Christmas Eve. Evergreen garlands bedeck posts around the Plaza. Crimson chile wreaths and strands of red and green chile lights are just a few of the New Mexico decorations.

Holiday performances of the *Messiah* by the Orchestra of Santa Fe, *Peter and the Wolf* by the Santa Fe Symphony, a performance of the Nutcracker ballet presented by the Pajarito Ballet, caroling, bell-ringing choirs and church concerts fill the calendar. Community groups as well as the Palace of the Governors present *Las Posadas,* the Spanish pageant of Mary and Joseph's search for shelter. Other groups perform *Los Pastores,* the nativity play of the shepherds.

Long before *Esquire* magazine decided this was "the right place to be," conquistadors, frontier merchants, artists and other hardy souls discovered Santa Fe. The city was founded in 1610 by Don Pedro de Peralta, before the Pilgrims arrived at Plymouth Rock.

The Plaza became the center of La Villa de Santa Fe. And it became the location for many upheavals and confrontations by the reconquering Spaniards, Pueblo Indians, Apaches, American troops and Confederate soldiers. It was a center for trade and raucous activity, including bullfights. But Santa Fe survived through the years and the diverse cultures learned to live together peacefully, giving the city its multicultural mix.

Today, many Pueblo Indians still travel to the Plaza, spreading their blankets under the portal of the Palace of the Governors to sell their hand-coiled pottery and silver and turquoise jewelry. Wrapped in heavy, bright blankets and shawls to ward off the winter chill, the Pueblo Indians offer authentic crafts much as they did when they sold to early traders. Many Pueblo Indians now work as scientists and technicians in nearby Los Alamos or are employed in other businesses in Santa Fe. But even modern-day Indians have strong cultural ties to the past. They maintain distinct languages within their pueblos and observe feast days and other special occasions with traditional dances.

During Christmas most pueblos celebrate with either an animal dance (deer or buffalo) or the ritualistic Matachines Dance. Observances vary from pueblo to pueblo, although most have special masses in their mission churches followed by a day of dancing. A steady drum beat and chant by the drummer sets a precise and synchronized rhythm for the costumed dancers. While the snow gently falls, the air fills with piñon and juniper smoke. Inside mud-plastered adobes, pueblo residents invite their friends to come to their table to share holiday bounty—chile, tamales, *chicos* and *sopa.*

Visitors may attend the dances as long as they respect the spiritual nature of the ceremony. Sometimes photography or sketching is prohibited, other times it is allowed for a fee.

If you're planning a weekend trip to Santa Fe, you'll find the city easily accessible from the north and south by I-25. The Santa Fe Chile Line offers transportation throughout the city in its modern trolleys. If you're coming from out of state, you can fly into Albuquerque International Airport, about an hour south of Santa Fe. From there you can take a local shuttle service or rent a car to Santa Fe. I-25 offers a pleasant, rolling drive up and down valleys and foothills. NM 14, a more scenic and leisurely route, will take you around the other side of the Sandía Mountains through an area that once thrived on mining.

Called the Turquoise Trail, NM 14 winds through Golden, Madrid and Cerrillos. For a while, it looked as though these villages might remain ghost towns. But within the past 20 years, these communities have grown as artists, shopkeepers and others seeking a quieter and less expensive lifestyle have moved in. It's not unusual to catch a bluegrass concert or a jazz festival during the summer in the Madrid ballpark. Melodramas also are staged at the Mine Shaft Theater. In December, Madrid has a holiday craft fair. Residents have restored some of the displays that were once part of a magnificent electric Christmas show in the 1930s.

The quiet town of Cerrillos becomes festive in June for its annual Fiesta Primavera, topped off with a wild firehose battle by local fire departments. Also, housed in an old opera house is Kludgit Sound, a recording studio that attracts many musicians to this tiny village year-round. As you travel along the Turquoise Trail, you can see faint ruts of an early wagon trail near the road.

Coming into Santa Fe from the south, you can follow another famous trail, the Old Santa Fe Trail, right to the Plaza, the perfect place to begin your Santa Fe weekend. The Plaza is nestled at the base of the Sangre de Cristo (blood of Christ) Mountains. Anchored on the north end is the Palace of the Governors, the oldest continuously used public building in the country. Today, you can walk through this authentic structure that is part of the Museum of New Mexico. Here you can learn about Santa Fe's history and the crucial role the Palace of the Governors played in its development. Operational old-time printing presses, stagecoaches and the room where Governor Lew Wallace finished *Ben Hur* are just a few of the attractions.

Besides informative exhibits, the Palace presents many special events in the patio.

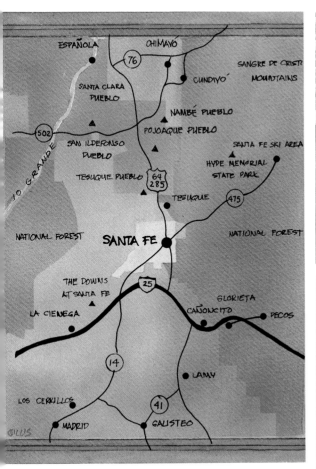

Top right—Snow blankets a home on Old Pecos Trail. ***Bottom right***—Los Pastores, *the shepherds' play performed at Rancho de las Golondrinas in La Cienega.*

Another community holiday event is *Las Posadas* on the Plaza. Spectators carry lit candles as a procession makes stops around the Plaza to sing traditional verses. A crowd favorite is the taunting, pointy-tailed red devil. After the procession, the crowd heads to the Palace patio where *luminarias,* hot chocolate and tasty *biscochitos* make a pleasant end to the event.

During summer months the Plaza bustles with activity. It's a gathering place for young punk rockers, cowboys and Hispanics. The elderly share an iron bench to discuss the day's events and feed the pigeons. Lawyers and shopkeepers meet to eat frito pies and

take in the action. Tourists laden with cameras wait for some excitement, such as when the Rubber Lady, a silent performance artist, makes an appearance, or when artist Tommy Macaione, who looks like Heidi's grandfather, sets up his easel.

Life is more easygoing in the winter, although shoppers scurry from store to store during the holiday rush. If you're visiting during December, you may want to stop at the First National Bank on the Plaza, where every year an elaborate model train chugs through a miniature New Mexico winter landscape with authentic-looking mountain terrain.

Anchored on the southeast end of the Plaza is historic La Fonda (the inn). Tourists as well as guests are welcome to explore the restaurant and many shops inside the heavy wooden doors that have welcomed celebrities and politicians through the decades.

Just down the street is St. Francis Cathedral, built by the French archbishop Jean Baptiste Lamy, who was the subject of Willa Cather's novel *Death Comes for the Archbishop*. This French Romanesque structure poses a contrast to the many adobe buildings in Santa Fe. Visitors may tour the cathedral, which was spruced up for its 100th anniversary celebration in 1986. Many Catholics will attend midnight mass there on Nochebuena, Christmas Eve.

A much smaller church, but equally fascinating, is the Loretto Chapel located near the cathedral. The "miraculous staircase" still puzzles visitors as they examine the beautiful winding wooden staircase that appears to stand without support. Adding to the appeal is the legend of a mysterious carpenter who built the staircase in answer to nuns' prayers for a way to reach the choir loft. Some like to think that St. Joseph, a carpenter, answered their prayers. This charming chapel provides an intimate setting for occasional concerts, including the annual holiday concert by the Santa Fe Women's Ensemble.

If you continue south a few more blocks along the Santa Fe Trail, you'll reach the oldest church and house in Santa Fe. Young and old enjoy ringing the historic bell at San Miguel Mission. Just behind the mission, you can visit the oldest house in Santa Fe, now a curio shop. Ask and you'll hear a few interesting ghost tales about the oldest house.

Just a bit farther south on the Santa Fe Trail is the Roundhouse, the country's newest capitol. It's quiet during the holidays, but the excitement returns when the Legislature goes into session in mid-January.

When you return to the Plaza, make sure to stop at the Fine Arts Museum, another division of the Museum of New Mexico. Built in a Pueblo style that resembles New Mexico mission churches, the structure is as spectacular as the exhibits on display. The museum has an extensive Southwestern collection and features permanent exhibits as well as contemporary shows. Frequently, classical concerts are presented in the adjoining St. Francis Auditorium, including the Chamber Music Festival every summer.

Half the fun of visiting Santa Fe is exploring the many shops, cafes and boutiques. Within a few blocks of the Plaza, you'll find shops and galleries tucked under the blue portals on Palace Avenue and in historic Sena Plaza. Along San Francisco Street you can wander into new mini malls where you'll find everything from fresh-baked cookies to designer clothing.

Two other areas in Santa Fe invite visitors to explore them on foot—Canyon Road and the developing Guadalupe Street area. For years many artists made their home in studios tucked away on Canyon Road. A few still live there, but you'll also find top-rate restaurants, quaint cafes and galleries along the narrow winding road, about five blocks southeast of the Plaza off Paseo de Peralta. Canyon Road hums with activity during the summer. In the winter, the pace is slower. It's relaxing to stop in a cafe for a quiet drink or cup of coffee while enjoying a roaring fireplace.

Guadalupe Street long has been a favorite with the local crowd. But during the past few years, more tourists are discovering the clothing shops, chic movie house, restaurants and other neighborhood attractions. The Santuario de Guadalupe, at the intersection of Guadalupe and Alameda streets, is a traditional, restored adobe church that houses special exhibits and presents classical and traditional Hispanic music performances.

Visitors to Santa Fe won't want to miss other outstanding museums that are just a short drive from downtown in the foothills on Camino Lejo. A nonprofit museum in a structure patterned after the Navajo hogan, the Wheelwright Museum of the American Indian presents exhibits of Native American art and culture throughout the year. If you visit during the Christmas holidays, don't forget to stop in the Case Trading Post downstairs where you'll find a Christmas tree decorated with Indian ornaments.

The Girard exhibit (donated by Alexander Girard) at the nearby Museum of International Folk Art is alone worth a trip to Santa Fe. A feast for the eyes, the displays of toys and other folk objects from around the world will delight both young and old. The state museum has other outstanding permanent exhibits on New Mexico folk art and frequently sponsors other special events, such as an annual children's holiday party.

Also along this road is the Laboratory of Anthropology and the state's newest museum, the Museum of Indian Arts and Culture. It uses the extensive research collections at the Laboratory of Anthropology to interpret and explain Southwest Indian culture. The Labo-

A scenic view of the Sangre de Cristos from an older residential area in southeastern Santa Fe.

ratory's collections include more than 50,000 pieces of pottery, basketry, weaving, jewelry, carvings and other Southwest crafts, and more than three million archaeological artifacts.

Nearby is the School of American Research. This fine institution offers lectures throughout the year, featuring speakers such as Jane Goodall.

Santa Fe also is home to St. John's College, companion to St. John's in Annapolis. The school presents many community lectures, concerts and special events. The College of Santa Fe, on the south end of town, welcomes visitors to drama performances at the Greer Garson Theatre and to art exhibits.

The Santa Fe Indian School also is based in the capital city. On the grounds, the Institute of American In-

dian Art Museum displays some of the best contemporary Indian art.

Santa Fe is known for its excellence in both visual and performing arts. During the winter months, you can go to performances by the Orchestra of Santa Fe, the Santa Fe Symphony, Theatre Intime (a subscription series of international theater, music and circus events), the New Mexico Repertory Theatre and the Santa Fe Community Theatre. The Center for Contemporary Arts offers film, exhibits, music and dance on the cutting edge.

If you've finished soaking in the culture and are ready to soak up some sun, head to the Santa Fe Ski Area, 16 miles northeast of town. Skiers will find just the lift they've been looking for—eight lifts, including

New Mexico's largest triple and the state's first quad chair lift. When you get to the top, you'll find spectacular views and 700 acres of powder. A ski school, cafeteria, rental shop and outside deck with a barbecue grill are a few of the amenities.

While you'll find a myriad of cultural events in the winter, summer is the city's busiest season. The world-renowned Santa Fe Opera performs in a magnificent outdoor theater, offering classical operas, as well as American and world premieres. During the summer months, the Santa Fe Chamber Music Festival brings together top contemporary composers and performers.

Outdoor enthusiasts also will find plenty to do in the summer months, including hiking, camping, fishing and river rafting. Horse-racing fans will discover that a stop at The Downs at Santa Fe is always a good bet. The track offers pari-mutuel quarter-horse and thoroughbred racing June through Labor Day.

If you're looking for a place to stay for your weekend, you'll have many choices. You can select from among luxury hotels, bed and breakfast establishments and economy motels.

The city teems with activity during the many special events that celebrate its multicultural heritage. Fiesta de Santa Fe, celebrated the weekend after Labor Day, commemorates the reentry of Gen. Don Diego de Vargas and his conquistadors when they settled New Mexico in 1692 after the Indian rebellion of 1680. A children's pet parade on Saturday morning, the historical/hysterical parade on Sunday afternoon, continuous entertainment on the Plaza and the Entrada (the reenactment of the conquistadors' entry into Santa Fe on horseback) are a few of the special events. To get things off to a festive start, Zozobra, the 40-foot puppet designed by artist Will Shuster, is burned amidst fireworks and the wild movements of a firedancer. Zozobra represents Old Man Gloom. Once people's troubles go up in smoke, they are free to have a joyous weekend. Fiesta ends on a more solemn and spiritual note with a candlelight procession to the Cross of the Martyrs.

Indian Market, generally the third weekend in August, attracts thousands to the city. Top Indian artists display their work under multicolored, canvas-covered booths. Prestigious awards attract artists from the Southwest and throughout the country. In late July, Hispanic craftsmen display weaving, woodcarving and other folk arts outside the Palace of the Governors at Spanish Market. And in early July cowboys and cowgirls converge on the capital city for the Rodeo de Santa Fe.

Year-round, visitors will find Santa Fe an ideal base for area excursions. Possible day trips include Bandelier National Monument, Rancho de las Golondrinas (an authentic recreation of a Hispanic village in nearby La Cienega), Pecos National Monument, the High Road to Taos and hot spring baths in Jémez and Ojo Caliente.

Let me warn you. Santa Fe is a lot like Camelot—it's hard to leave her in winter, spring, summer or fall.

Santa Fe is the oldest capital in the country. Tourism and state government are the city's major industries. A longtime haven for artists, the visual and performing arts flourish here. Streets converge at the Plaza at the end of the Santa Fe Trail. Within easy walking distance from the Plaza are gourmet restaurants, galleries and museums. The Sangre de Cristo Mountains provide a spectacular backdrop to the city and offer outdoor recreational opportunities.

POPULATION: 53,000.

ELEVATION: 7,000 feet.

CLIMATE: The average high temperature in July is 85 degrees with an average low of 56 degrees at night. In January the average high is 42 degrees with an average low of 18 degrees at night.

PRECIPITATION: Yearly rainfall is 14 inches. Yearly snowfall in town is 32 inches.

SPECIAL EVENTS: Fiesta de Santa Fe in September, Indian Market in August, Spanish Market in July, Spring Arts New Mexico, Rodeo de Santa Fe in July and Christmas celebrations.

NEARBY ATTRACTIONS: Santa Fe Ski Area, Pecos National Monument, Bandelier National Monument, the Downs at Santa Fe, Rancho de las Golondrinas in La Cienega, High Road to Taos, Hyde Memorial State Park and Pecos Wilderness.

The Big Ditch Park, once Main Street before it was destroyed in a flood, offers visitors an attractive retreat in downtown Silver City.

Silver City

by Emily Drabanski

For centuries people in search of riches set out to the mountains surrounding the Silver City area in southwestern New Mexico. Early Indians found their treasure in the rich deposits of turquoise and in the bountiful hunting grounds. By 1840 the Spanish were digging for copper in an area east of what they called the San Vicente Cienega, at the site of present day Silver City.

In 1870 prospectors discovered silver, and the rush was on. In 10 months the newly named Silver City boomed from a single cabin to 80 buildings. When silver prices crashed in 1893, most other mining towns were abandoned to become ghost towns. But an optimistic citizenry, who built their homes out of brick, stayed where they had firmly planted their roots.

Weekend visitors today will find an area rich in tales of the Wild West, remnants of ancient Indian cultures, ghost towns and hundreds of acres of unspoiled wilderness. The only problem may be the nagging urge to stay longer to see everything.

Silver City is easily accessible from I-10, a major southern artery, via NM 90 from Lordsburg or via US 180 from Deming. Travelers from the north can drive south on I-25 past Truth or Consequences and then west across scenic NM 152 through the Black Range.

Mining continues as the economic base of Silver City, although it is copper, not silver, that is mined. The Phelps Dodge mine in Tyrone, south of Silver City, offers tours, and visitors can view the Santa Rita open-pit mine from a pullover off NM 152 east of Silver City.

But, if you just come to visit the mines, you'll find you're only scratching the surface of an area that invites exploration. To help you on your hunt of the area's treasures, the Silver City Chamber of Commerce publishes a newspaper featuring four historic scenic loop tours with detailed directions and maps that correspond to brown numbered signs in the area.

These tours are highly recommended and will help you get a sense of the Wild West. For example, Billy-the-Kid buffs can see the site of his boyhood home, the place where he was jailed, the site of the Star Hotel where he waited on tables and his mother's grave. Of equal interest are the stories of Gerónimo, Ben Lilly, Judge Roy Bean and Butch Cassidy, who also left their mark.

Gough Park with its lovely gazebo is the focal point for city celebrations. A cowboy breakfast in the park kicks off Frontier Days on the Fourth of July, followed by three days of wild bronc riding, bazaars, barbecues, parades, fireworks and art shows. The city celebrates mining days on Labor Day weekend with similar gusto.

While visiting downtown, walk through the archway sign off Market and Bullard streets to descend to what was once the city's main street and is now the Big Ditch Park. During a series of floods from 1895-1906, Main Street was swept away by walls of water up to 12 feet tall, dropping the street level by 55 feet. Today visitors can stroll across charming footbridges and follow shaded paths that hug the ditch, where water still flows.

If you think only the rough and tough left their mark on Silver City, just look down the city's streets to spot elegant Victorian homes. And if you always wanted to peek inside one, stop by the Silver City Museum at 312 Broadway SW. Climb the winding staircase to the tiny cupola to get a bird's-eye view of the city. There's no charge to tour this wonderful museum filled with interpretive exhibits about the Mimbres Indians,

Spanish miners, Apaches, prospectors and those who brought the fineries that marked frontier Victoriana.

The museum hosts a variety of events, such as an ice cream social on the Fourth of July and a Victorian Christmas party. It also offers an excellent free guide to the city's historic districts.

Western New Mexico University Museum, off US 180 and Alabama Street, has an outstanding collection of distinctive black-on-white Mimbres pottery, made by the Indians who lived in the Mimbres River Valley from about A.D. 900 to 1150.

Those interested in ancient Indian cultures should visit the Gila Cliff Dwellings National Monument, 44 miles north of Silver City on NM 15. It's a scenic drive through rolling piñon- and juniper-studded hills, then through the fragrant, towering pines as the road snakes alongside the Gila River. Be prepared though for a slow drive, up the narrow, two-lane road with frequent hairpin turns. Trailers more than 20 feet long shouldn't come this way and are advised to travel on NM 35, reached from NM 152 at San Lorenzo.

If you drive via NM 15, you'll find several scenic pullovers and picnic areas. Developed and primitive campgrounds are available in the Gila River Recreation Area. In Gila Hot Springs, three miles south of the Gila Visitor Center, there are cabins and a trailer park. You may want to pack a lunch, since the drive to the monument's visitor center is about two hours each way, and it takes another hour to walk the one-mile, self-guided loop to the ruins.

The visitor center will help orient you to the ruins and is a must stop for those who need permits to hike or ride horses into the backcountry. The Gila Cliff Dwellings are open year-round; hours vary from season to season. Contact the Gila Visitor Center at (505) 536-9461 or Route 11, Box 100, Silver City, NM 88061 for current information.

From the visitor center, take the road west to the monument. Here the trail to the cliff dwellings zig-zags up 175 feet above the canyon to a world inhabited by the Mogollón Indians more than 700 years ago. As you walk along the path to these unusual ruins tucked beneath the cliffs, you can experience the same sense of wonder that Adolph Bandelier felt in 1884 when he discovered several caves.

After exploring the cliff dwellings, you may choose to return to town or to stay and enjoy the outdoors. The Gila National Forest offers some of the best fishing and hunting in the state. For the fishing enthusiast,

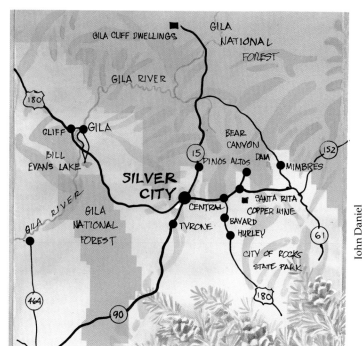

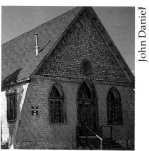

Above right—The desert garden exhibits a variety of cacti at the City of Rocks State Park. ***Bottom center***—The Catwalk offers a breathtaking hike through Whitewater Canyon. ***Bottom right***—The adobe Methodist-Episcopal Church was built by the Hearst family in 1898. It now houses the Grant County Art Guild.

Bear Canyon Dam, Bill Evans Lake and Lake Roberts are all within 45 minutes of Silver City, providing rainbow trout in the winter and bass, crappie, bluegill and catfish in the summer.

Many people come to the area to bird-watch. Myra McCormick at Bear Mountain Guest Ranch offers guided bird-watching trips. Or if you'd like to view on your own, just take a minute to stop and listen. Yep, that's really a turkey you hear gobbling off in the distance.

On your trip back on NM 15, you can stop in the early gold-mining town of Pinos Altos, nestled in the tall pines six miles north of Silver City. A group of 49ers drifting back from California found gold here in 1859. It became a rough and tumble town of gold bonanzas and Apache raids. To learn more about the local lore, stop at the Pinos Altos Museum, housed in a log cabin—Grant County's first private school, built around 1866. Proprietor George Schafer offers a wealth of oral history.

Another interesting stop is the ¾-scale reproduction of the Santa Rita del Cobre Fort and Trading Post. The original was built at the Santa Rita copper mine in 1804 to protect the area from Apaches. Other points of interest include the adobe Methodist-Episcopal Church built by the Hearst family, the McDonald Cabin and the Judge Roy Bean Store site. The Buckhorn Saloon and Opera House offers fine dining and melodramas in a Wild West setting. For those who'd like to spend the night, there are cabins.

Once back in Silver City, you can explore further in any direction. One day trip is a loop tour that begins east on US 180, then turns south at Central. As you drive south on US 180, you'll experience the desert, a striking contrast from your trip into the forest. Turn left when you reach NM 61.

You'll see the entrance on the left to the City of Rocks State Park about 10 minutes later. Here, as the name implies, gigantic rocks create an eerie and awesome geologic wonder. There are picnic tables and a small desert garden.

Continue driving northeast on NM 61, and just a bit farther on this road is the Faywood Hot Springs, contained in stone and concrete pools. Remnants of an old bathhouse remain.

As you continue on NM 61, you'll drive through the fertile Mimbres Valley, once inhabited by the artistic

101

Mimbres Indians. During the harvest season, you can stop at roadside stands to buy fresh produce and honey. In San Lorenzo, head east on NM 152.

If you didn't travel this way into Silver City, this will give you a chance to see the Santa Rita open-pit copper mine. From here you can see a rock outcropping to the east, which residents call the Kneeling Nun. The legend claims a nun was in love with a Spanish soldier and turned to stone when she knelt to pray. Also en route to Silver City as you travel NM 152 is Fort Bayard, built in 1866 for the buffalo soldiers of the 125th U.S. Colored Infantry, an all-black regiment.

There's another recommended day trip. By heading northwest on US 180 you reach Glenwood, a small town that attracts fishermen and hunters; the Catwalk, a spectacular hike along the Whitewater River, and Mogollón, an old mining town. If you plan to take the extended loop back to Silver City through the forest via NM 159 east and Mogollón (advisable only in the warmer dry months), then Glenwood is your last chance to stop for gas.

Take a short drive east on the Whitewater Canyon Road to reach the Glenwood Hatchery. The Catwalk, one of the area's most spectacular attractions, is another five miles farther. Check road conditions, however. You'll have to drive across water twice. Usually it is shallow, but not always.

The Catwalk offers one of the most exciting hikes in the state. Where else can you walk suspended along the sheer rock face while white water roars beneath your feet? The trail will take you crisscross along the river over a series of wooden, metal and suspension bridges. You'll need almost two hours to complete the trip. This may be a full day for you, and you may choose to return to Silver City.

To travel the extended loop, return to US 180 and drive north to NM 159 and Mogollón, a well-preserved old mining town.

A word of caution: the route to Mogollón offers incredible views, but it also is a narrow, steep, two-lane road with fast switchbacks—a real white-knuckle drive for flatlanders. This road will take you through the high country past Snow Lake and Wall Lake, both popular fishing and camping spots. There are several alternate routes in the high country—all along rougher roads. Consult a forest service map and residents to make your choice.

Chances are, most visitors will get only a taste of the Silver City area on their weekend visit and will be tempted to return. The Gila National Forest alone encompasses more than 3 million acres; one-fourth is designated wilderness or primitive areas. The largest is the 438,360-acre Gila Wilderness, promoted by conservationist Aldo Leopold and set aside as the first such area in the U.S. in 1924.

Silver City's economy is based on mining, ranching, agriculture, education and tourism. It is the gateway to the Gila National Forest and Wilderness, a region of scenic beauty in the high mountains. It is an area rich in the history of the Apache, Spanish and the Anglo pioneers.

POPULATION: City, 10,807. County, 26,204.

ELEVATION: 5,895 feet above sea level.

TERRAIN: Mountainous with desert to the south.

CLIMATE: Winters are mild with temperatures of 49 degrees during the day and 24 degrees at night. Summers are warm with average temperatures of 87 degrees during the day and cool nighttime temperatures of 59 degrees.

PRECIPITATION: Annual average is 15.6 inches.

NEARBY ATTRACTIONS: The Catwalk, City of Rocks State Park, Gila Cliff Dwellings National Monument, the Glenwood Hatchery, Lake Roberts, Mogollón, Silver City Museum, the Big Ditch Park, Old Tyrone/Phelps Dodge Open Pit Mine and Mill, Pinos Altos, the Santa Rita Open Pit Mine and Chino Smelter, Snow Lake and Western New Mexico University.

Wildflowers provide a golden carpet for the San Agustín Plains west of Socorro.

Socorro & Belén

by Joyce Mendel

S ocorro, flanked by the Río Grande on the east and Socorro Peak on the west, lies in a semidesert valley surrounded by vast open spaces. Only about 9,000 residents live in the city, yet it receives thousands of visitors annually drawn by the Bosque del Apache National Wildlife Refuge, 18 miles south of Socorro. The refuge is winter home for tens of thousands of migratory birds, including the rare whooping crane.

Located 74 miles south of Albuquerque and 147 miles north of Las Cruces, Socorro is easily accessible in a north-south direction from I-25. Coming from the east, take US 380 to its intersection with I-25 at San An-

tonio, 10 miles south of Socorro. US 60 winds into town from the west.

Traffic and bustle predominate along Socorro's California Street (US 85-60), lined with motels, restaurants and stores. But once off that artery, a tranquil, slower pace takes over. Along the eastern edge of town, cottonwoods and fields line the river lowlands. To the west, Socorro's plaza has a central position. Narrow winding streets and 19th-century adobe buildings north of the plaza recall days of Spanish and Mexican rule. Brick homes of the late Victorian period, built by prosperous residents during Socorro's mining boom, stand sedately along Church and McCutcheon streets, a few blocks southwest of the plaza.

But in earlier days, raiding Indians and rowdy miners upset the town's tranquility. Piro Indians originally settled the lands. One of the Piro pueblos provided Oñate's Spanish expedition much-needed supplies on its northward trek from Mexico in 1598. A grateful Oñate named the assisting pueblo Socorro, meaning "succor" or "help."

Spaniards founded a mission in the area in 1626, dedicated to Nuestra Señora del Socorro (Our Lady of Help). But the church and Piro pueblos were abandoned in 1680 when Pueblo Indians in northern New Mexico revolted against Spanish rule. The Spanish and most of the Piros fled south, the Piros never to return. According to legend, mission priests buried a silver communion rail and silver vessels before they left. The objects were never recovered.

Although Spanish colonizers resettled parts of the central Río Grande Valley in the 1690s, raiding Apaches prevented habitation of the Socorro area for about 100 years. A group of families finally settled the area and were awarded the Socorro Land Grant about 1816. They built a church, probably at the site of the previous looted and burned mission, naming it San Miguel.

Catholic services are still conducted at the church, open to the public. Carved wooden beams span the massive five-foot-thick adobe walls of the church's nave, which is flanked by two bell towers. Some of the area's leading citizens of the past lie buried beneath the four subfloors. For a better sense of the church's history, you can view artifacts discovered during San Miguel's 1974 renovation in the church office.

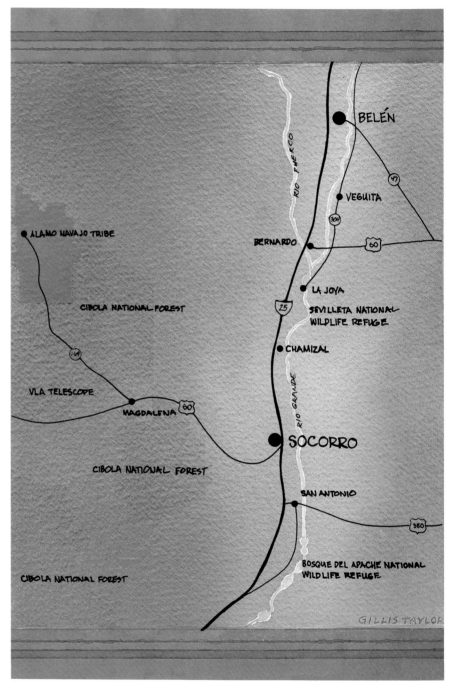

You'll find Old San Miguel Mission by turning west on Calle de San Miguel off California Street, then right on El Camino Real. The first weekend in August a fiesta celebrates the church's saint's day with booths, entertainment, nighttime dancing and special masses.

Apache raids menaced Socorro settlers until the 1880s, when the railroad's coming led to increased safety and prosperity. Socorro boomed in the 1880s and early 1890s. Silver was mined from nearby mountains, the population climbed to about 5,000 and the Socorro Vigilantes formed to maintain order in one of the wildest towns in the West. Many of the new residents left at the turn of the century, however, after the price of silver plunged.

Growth did not begin again until the 1930s, although a major building, the Val Verde Hotel, was constructed in 1919 in Spanish mission revival style. The renovated former hotel, at 203 Manzanares Avenue, now houses a restaurant that retains many features of the early hotel dining room. Shops and offices fill other first-story rooms.

Although Socorro treasures its past, much of the city's economy is based on modern technology. On Socorro's west side, at the western terminus of College Avenue, the New Mexico Institute of Mining and Technology and its adjacent industrial park edge up toward Socorro Peak. The campus is a garden of grass and shade trees interspersed with white, red-roofed, Spanish colonial-style buildings. The rolling lawns of an 18-hole golf course, open to the public, extend the school grounds.

The institute, commonly referred to as Tech, offers approximately 1,200 students small classes and close interaction with faculty and other researchers. Founded in 1889, Tech provides education in earth and basic sciences and in mining and petroleum engineering. Researchers work on such technological frontiers as welding metals together with explosives and improving methods for oil and gas recovery.

When visiting Tech, stop at the Mineral Museum in Workman Center to see displays of fluorescent minerals, New Mexico fossils, including a mastodon jaw about 2.5 million years old, and sizable specimens of other minerals.

The annual Hilton Open tees off at Tech's golf course each June. In Macy Center, at the campus' northwestern edge, classical and popular performers entertain during a performing art series September through April.

Several celebrations take place in Socorro during spring and late summer. A Mother's Day weekend Springfest at the plaza includes a parade, food and crafts booths and a quilt sale. On Labor Day weekend, Western traditions come alive at Socorro County's annual fair and rodeo.

In addition to the Bosque del Apache, other interesting trips can be made from Socorro. Fifty-one miles to the west sprawls the Very Large Array (VLA), the world's most powerful radio telescope and part of the National Radio Astronomy Observatory. Follow the sign on Socorro's California Street that points the way to US 60. The highway climbs the southern end of the Socorro Mountains and winds 26 miles to Magdalena, the only community between Socorro and the VLA.

Magdalena, settled in the late 19th century, started as an adjunct to the mining town of Kelly, a few miles to the south in the Magdalena Mountains. But a railroad spur built between Magdalena and Socorro in 1884 made Magdalena a cowboy town. Magdalena was the end of the trail during days of big cattle drives through the Plains of San Agustín 20 miles to the west. For a while, more cattle were shipped from Magdalena than any other place in the country. Now the former train depot houses Magdalena's city hall.

Kelly, a town that began with two mining claims in 1866, has been a ghost town since 1945. To reach it, turn south at the ranger station in Magdalena. The town thrived in the 1880s when lead and silver were mined and in the early 20th century with the mining of zinc.

Farther west on US 60, about 20 miles from Magdalena, you'll come to the brow of a hill looking down on the Plains of San Agustín, a huge, flat, mountain-ringed basin 60 miles long and up to 40 miles wide. A vast cattle and sheep industry once existed on the grasslands, but today the view most resembles a scene from science fiction, with 27 gigantic, dish-shaped antennas, each 82 feet in diameter and weighing 230 tons, strung out along the plains.

The road from US 60 to the VLA Visitor Center lies a short distance from the base of the hill. You can see a 15-minute slide program and an exhibit at the center. A self-guided walking tour begins at the center's back door.

Radio signals collected from each antenna forming the VLA go to a central computer where they're combined to form detailed pictures of faint objects in the universe. Every few months the antennas are moved to different locations along three 13-mile-long radial arms arranged in a Y-shaped configuration.

The VLA lies at an altitude of 7,000 feet, so winter snow sometimes obscures the white antennas. You may want to call before making the trip (772-4255).

Another side trip from Socorro takes you north 43 miles to Belén. If you'd like a leisurely alternative to I-25, exit at Bernardo and drive north on NM 116 west of the Bernardo gas station. The highway takes you into Belén and passes the Bernardo Waterfowl Area, a state refuge.

Belén, settled by the Spanish in 1741, became a railroading center in the 1880s. From 1910 to 1939, railroad passengers dined at the mission-style Harvey House across from the depot. They were served by white-aproned waitresses known as Harvey Girls, who lived in upstairs rooms. The Belén Chamber of Commerce and the Valencia County Museum have now settled into first-floor rooms of the renovated Harvey House, 104 North First Street. The museum includes a room furnished in the style of a Harvey Girl's bedroom, with a white brass bed, washstand, rocking chair and corner trunk.

For a glimpse at Hispanic farm life in the nearby Jarales area, turn east from Belén's Main Street to NM 309 (Reinken Avenue). Several miles down, turn south at NM 109 (Jarales Road). Past two sets of railroad tracks, on the west side of the road, you'll come to the P&M Chavez Farm Museum. Pablo and Manuela Chavez still farm their land while running the home-based private museum. A barn holds antique cars along with 19th- and early 20th-century farm equipment, much of it used at one time by Jarales farmers. Parts of the Chavez home and shed are furnished as a bedroom and kitchen of earlier times, and antique furnishings from around the world cram the museum. Call in advance to be sure it's open (864-8354).

The Immaculate Conception Church and Museum in the village of Tomé preserve Hispanic religious traditions. To reach it, return to NM 309, going east to NM 47. Tomé, about 6 miles north, was settled in 1739. Turn west at the small sign for the church and museum. The one-room museum lies adjacent to the small 241-year-old adobe church. The museum displays old, carved-wood santos and other church-associated objects. Informational signs and photographs tell the parish's history.

If you have time to wander, the Socorro-Belén area has other sights to suit your interests, such as the ghost town of Riley, La Joya Waterfowl Area, old Hispanic villages along NM 304 (part of the old Royal Highway from Santa Fe into Mexico) and Senator Willie M. Chavez State Park beside the Río Grande near Belén.

Socorro and Belén lie in the expansive Río Grande Valley south of Albuquerque, each with longstanding Hispanic roots. Belén is a center for farming and ranching. The road NM 47 between Albuquerque and Belén is sprinkled with the Hispanic villages of Peralta, Valencia and Tomé that grew along the old supply route to Mexico, El Camino Real. Socorro, in a rich mining area, is now home to the New Mexico Institute of Mining and Technology.

POPULATION: Socorro, 9,300. Belén, 8,300.

ELEVATION: Socorro, 4,620 feet above sea level. Belén, 4,840 feet above sea level.

CLIMATE: July temperatures average 95 degrees in the day and 64 degrees at night. In January daytime temperatures average 52 degrees in the day and 24 degrees at night. Those are averages for Socorro. Temperatures are generally several degrees cooler in Belén.

PRECIPITATION: Rainfall averages 8.8 inches per year in Socorro. Belén generally receives 10 inches per year.

SPECIAL EVENTS: Socorro Springfest in May, San Miguel Fiesta in Socorro in August, Hilton Open Golf Tournament in June, Socorro County Fair in September, Chile Chase Golf Tournament in Socorro in September, Annual 49ers Day in October at NMIMT, Candy Cane Parade in December in Socorro, St. Patrick's Balloon Rally in March in Belén, Río Valley Festival-Triathlon in June in Belén, Valencia County Fair in August and Our Lady of Belén Fiestas in August.

NEARBY ATTRACTIONS: Bosque del Apache National Wildlife Refuge, VLA National Radio Astronomy Observatory, Harvey House in Belén, P&M Chavez Farm Museum, Immaculate Conception Church and Museum in Tomé, San Miguel Mission in Socorro, Sevilleta National Wildlife Refuge and Senator Willie M. Chavez State Park.

BOSQUE DEL APACHE

Joan McCampbell Sleeter

A Bird-watcher's Paradise

From mid-November through early February, billowing clouds of snow geese ascend each dawn from the Bosque del Apache's marshes amid a din of flapping wings and piercing calls. Twilight flights against a background of multicolored sky and isolated hills are equally dramatic, as ducks, geese and cranes return to roost.

The Bosque del Apache National Wildlife Refuge was established along the south-central Río Grande in 1939 to develop and protect habitat for waterfowl and other wildlife. Last year about 10,000 sandhill cranes, 10 whooping cranes, 40,000 snow geese and 16,000 ducks wintered at the 57,191-acre refuge. Summer brings fewer birds but different varieties. Besides 295 bird species, more than 400 species of mammals, reptiles and amphibians flourish on refuge acreage.

A 15-mile loop driving tour meanders past fields with feeding geese and cranes, woods with watchful deer and ponds with ducks and egrets. You might hear coyotes howling in the hills or see one lurking in a cornfield. Two viewing stands and short walking trails give you alternative ways to see the wildlife, and three upland wildernesses are open for day hikes.

The endangered whooping crane, North America's largest bird, comes to the refuge because of an innovative program begun in 1975. Trying to save the endangered species, scientists have been placing whooping crane eggs in sandhill cranes' nests at the sandhills' Idaho nesting grounds. Young whoopers migrate to New Mexico's Río Grande Valley with their foster parents each fall. A white, nearly five-foot-tall whooping crane is easy to spot among the smaller, slate gray sandhills.

The Bosque del Apache is about eight miles south of San Antonio on NM 1. A visitor center is across the road from the refuge's main entrance.

For more information, write or call Bosque del Apache National Wildlife Refuge, PO Box 1246, Socorro, NM 87801, 835-1828.

—**Joyce Mendel**

The majestic Sangre de Cristo Mountains near Taos dominate the landscape.

Tony Chiodo

Taos

by Judy Romero

A ll the wild inconsistencies, breathtaking scenery and cultural diversity of New Mexico converge in Taos and the surrounding countryside. On a weekend tour you can choose anything from history, ancient cultures, green mountains, trout fishing or foot-stomping dancing to the best in Western music. Or you can squeeze them all into one weekend if you choose.

Where else can you raft down a whitewater river during the day and enjoy chamber music at night? Or experience world-class skiing by day and in the evening savor a bowl of steaming hot chile while listening to the strains of a flamenco guitarist? Or spend a lazy summer afternoon wandering winding dirt roads to discover a wonderful restaurant or outstanding gallery tucked in an old adobe building? Taos, in northern New Mexico, is a perfect place to get away from it all.

For nearly a century, artists have tried to capture the shimmering light of Taos. Many visitors wish they were artists once they see this high-altitude city with its ancient adobe walls, vaulted blue skies and dancing aspens for the first time. If you're not an artist, bring a camera to carry home the visual drama of the mountain communities.

Driving north from Santa Fe on NM 68, you will round a mountain curve and marvel at the panorama of mountains. Veiled in blue haze, the mountains rise over the sprawling Taos Valley, sleeping giants left from the prehistoric age of volcanoes. The Río Grande

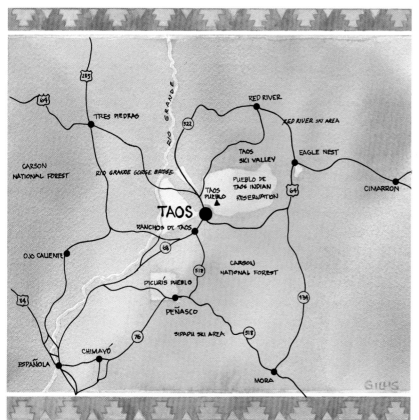

Top right—The Taos Pueblo attracts visitors year-round. **Bottom right**—The Plaza is in the heart of downtown Taos.

Gorge splits the valley in a jagged crack. So many visitors have tied up highway traffic at the top of the hill that a rest stop has been provided, with a perfect vantage point for taking pictures.

If you come from the south over the High Road from Truchas and Peñasco, your first glimpse of Taos will be of ancient mountains looming over the valley. From the east on US 64 you'll wind through aspen-lined canyons. From the west via Tres Piedras and from the north on NM 522 every curve opens onto wide vistas.

The main must-see attractions in Taos for short trips are the Plaza area, Taos Pueblo, the Río Grande Gorge Bridge and the massive walls of San Francisco de Asís Church in Ranchos de Taos.

Taos Pueblo draws more visitors per year than any other local site. The Indian pueblo's traditional apartmentlike adobe structures are part of one of the oldest still-occupied human settlements in the country. Visits in the late summer or fall can provide a lesson in adobe construction, when residents replaster portions of the ancient buildings before winter snows arrive.

Indian bread bakes in outdoor *hornos* (ovens) heated by fragrant piñon wood as tourists buy traditional arts and crafts at the pueblo. Throughout the year, feast days such as the San Gerónimo fiesta on September 30 feature dances, early-morning races and pole climbing games.

The Taos Indians jealously guard their independence and are proud of their government, which consists of a governor and council. Since some of their income comes from tourists, they charge parking and photography fees.

A visitor center at the pueblo entrance is open all summer, with Indian arts and crafts, a video program about Pueblo life and information on Indian ceremonials. Call 758-9593 for information.

The smaller pueblo of Picurís near Peñasco was said

109

to be nine stories tall when the Spaniards first visited in 1598. A visitor center and museum, the Church of San Lorenzo and the old pueblo excavation are open to visitors. Picnic areas offer rainbow and brown trout fishing for a fee.

Eastern artists discovered Taos in the early 1900s and founded one of the first Western art colonies. You can relive those days by visiting the Fechin House, where Russian artist Nicolai Fechin built an adobe home in Russian style; the Blumenschein House, home of Ernest Blumenschein, one of the founders of the famous Taos Society of Artists, and Las Palomas, the grand adobe compound of famous art patroness Mabel Dodge Luhan, where renowned artists and writers such as D.H. Lawrence, Georgia O'Keeffe, Aldous Huxley and Willa Cather frequently met.

The days of D.H. Lawrence are remembered at La Fonda, a hotel on the Plaza, and the Lawrence ranch north of Taos. Reserve a couple of hours for a drive to the ranch and back.

The Harwood Foundation, located in a historical building within walking distance of the Plaza, houses a unique community library, an art gallery, children's library and art archives. The Harwood has a large collection of books about the history and archaeology of the north and about the early Taos artists.

If art galleries are your main interest, they are tucked into every nook and cranny of the winding streets of Taos. Last count was around 60, but it's ever changing.

Early Spanish and frontier life is recalled at Gov. Charles Bent's and Kit Carson's homes, both museums, just off the Plaza. The Martínez Hacienda on Ranchitos Road, a five-minute drive from the plaza, is a beautifully restored hacienda with 21 rooms and two courtyards, built like a fort and self-sufficient in every way. It was the home of merchant Don Antonio Severino Martínez, father of the famous—and controversial—Padre Martínez. It's one of the last of the great haciendas of the Southwest. The hacienda has changing displays of early Spanish colonial life.

Long John Dunn was one of the colorful, wild characters drawn to northern New Mexico by the gold boom of the late 1800s. He arrived just ahead of the law and settled in Elizabethtown, now a ghost town near Red River, where he made his living at the gambling tables of the wild little gold rush town.

He later moved to Taos, married a local woman and settled down slightly to run the Taos stagecoach line and a toll bridge. Shops now fill his rambling house along a boardwalk behind the Plaza.

Dunn had a woodpile just outside his kitchen door. His woodpile is famous because he decided to hide some dynamite sticks in it and forgot to inform his wife. The resulting explosion in the kitchen stove is one of the stories you'll hear if you take Char Graebner's walking tour around the Plaza. The tours are easygoing for the most reluctant walker and cover most of the historic places in the center of town. Graebner also leads tours to artists' studios.

The Taos Chamber of Commerce runs an information booth on the Plaza throughout summer. During fall and winter the chamber office, next to the Indian Hills Inn on Pueblo Sur, can give you information on everything from a one-day tour of Taos County to a week-long camping trip.

The Río Grande Gorge Basin, eight miles west of US 64, leaps the chasm of the gorge 650 feet above the river. You won't see the gorge until you're on it, and the canyon walls drop away beneath the second-highest suspension bridge in the nation. A picnic area and campgrounds offer an opportunity to enjoy the spectacular scenery beside the bridge.

Layers of history can be read in the rock walls of the Río Grande Gorge. You can view the bottom of the gorge and camp along the river by taking the Carson Bridge road south of Taos on NM 570. The road is primitive, its one lane climbing down the side of the gorge. You can drive to the same place through Pilar.

Another attraction you won't want to miss is the world-famous Millicent Rogers Museum four miles north of Taos. Here you can see more than 50 pots that renowned San Ildefonso potter María Martínez and her family made and saved for their own personal collection. The museum also presents art and history-related events year-round.

The San Francisco de Asís church at Ranchos de Taos, just south of Taos, is one of the most photographed churches in the nation. Famous for its massive, buttressed adobe walls and graceful towers, it invites photographers and artists at any hour of the day. It also contains a "miracle painting" that changes in the dark.

Archaeologists work each summer on the excavation of an ancient pueblo near Fort Burgwin southeast of Taos on NM 518. The old fort includes a museum and weekly lectures on prehistory during the summer. Call first (758-8322) before visiting.

The Enchanted Circle tour, a 100-mile scenic loop

A glistening adobe wall in Taos.

drive that begins and ends in Taos, will give you an overall view of four mountain towns and the breathtaking scenery around them. The trip can take from half a day to three days, depending on how long you spend in each place.

Beginning in Taos, drive east on US 64 through Taos Canyon, over Palo Flechado Pass, past the DAV Viet-nam Veterans Memorial Chapel. Turn off NM 434 and loop through Angel Fire, a four-season resort offering golfing, tennis, fishing, and horseback riding. Green mountains invite picnicking and biking in the summer and skiing and snowmobiling in the winter.

Continuing on US 64, you'll feel as if you're on top of the world at Eagle Nest, with its sprawling lake and view of snow-capped Mt. Wheeler, the highest point in New Mexico (13,161 feet). Follow NM 38 past the Elizabethtown ruins and drop dizzily into the deep canyon filled with Red River's shops, restaurants and year-round fun: go-carts and jeep rides in the summer, skiing and snowmobiling in the winter.

Continue on to the village of Questa, famous for its honey, and back on NM 522 towards Taos. At the junction just north of Taos take NM 150 to the Taos Ski Valley and back.

Some of the top names in jazz perform at the ski valley, and quiet chamber music concerts lull audiences on summer evenings. Skiers from around the world pack the resort in the winter.

Eagle Nest Lake offers the best in fishing and water sports, including windsurfing. A brilliant fireworks display reflects itself in the lake on the Fourth of July.

All of these mountain villages bustle with skiers in the winter, lively entertainment and the best in New Mexican food and Texas-style barbecue.

Angel Fire is famous for its chamber music program, and Red River offers Old West festivals. Horseback or jeep rides to see the golden aspens are available in the fall.

Other nearby outdoor attractions in northern New Mexico include ski areas, mountain lakes and streams, hot springs, campgrounds and hundreds of miles of backpacking and hiking trails.

Events fill the calendar in Taos and surroundings all year. One of the best weekends to visit Taos is late September for the annual wool festival in Kit Carson Park. The festival brings together Colorado and New Mexico wool growers and fashion artists for two days of fleece contests, history and food featuring lamb.

Children and adults love the touchable angora goats, rabbits, llamas and sheep on display. The festival is sponsored by the Mountain and Valley Wool Association.

May and October mark the two annual art festivals in Taos, with more receptions and special events than you'll be able to take in. Taos also hosts a balloon festival the last weekend in October. November begins the season of snow sports.

Christmas turns Taos into an enchanted garden of lights with *farolitos* (candles in sand-laden paper bags) lining the Plaza buildings. *Las Posadas,* the reenactment of Mary and Joseph's search for lodgings, takes place nine days before Christmas. Church bells and candlelight processions fill the cold, wintery nights.

Red River has its annual Winter Carnival in January, and Angel Fire whoops it up with shovel races down the mountain during Winterfest Weekend in February.

April begins the whitewater season for rafters on the Río Grande, and many visitors come to watch the experts fight the rapids. Red River celebrates Gold Rush Days in May, and Taos presents a soaring festival for gliders and a rodeo in June.

Red River celebrates the Fourth of July for four days, and Taos has a three-day street party the last weekend in July for the feast days of Santa Ana and Santiago.

Taos is internationally known for art and skiing. It is a year-round resort community with easy access to the Río Grande Gorge and the mountains. Its population is a fascinating mixture of artists, people involved in tourism-related businesses, ranchers and retirees. The Taos Pueblo is nearby and is one of the oldest in the Southwest.

POPULATION: Approximately 4,000.

ELEVATION: 6,950 feet above sea level.

CLIMATE: There are four definite seasons. Winters are cold with highs of 40 degrees in January and lows of 10 degrees at night. Summers are pleasant with an average high temperature of 87 degrees in July and a low of about 50 degrees at night.

PRECIPITATION: Annual average is 12.1 inches.

SPECIAL EVENTS: Annual spring and fall art festivals, rodeo and glider festival in June, Taos Fiesta de Santiago y Santa Ana in late July, annual Taos Pueblo Powwow in July, San Gerónimo Day in late September.

NEARBY ATTRACTIONS: Taos Pueblo, Río Grande Gorge Bridge, San Francisco de Asis Church in Ranchos de Taos, Taos Ski Valley, DAV Vietnam Veterans Memorial Chapel in Angel Fire, Picurís Pueblo, D.H. Lawrence Ranch, Eagle Nest, Red River, Angel Fire.

The sun sets over Elephant Butte Reservoir, the largest lake in New Mexico.

Truth or Consequences

by Marc Sani

Apaches led Spanish explorers to hot springs at the place now called Truth or Consequences. Today, centuries later, people are still coming to "take the waters."

Garlon and Faye Gill are true believers in the waters of Truth or Consequences—T or C as many call it. "We moved here from Texas in 1982, when my arthritis was so bad," said Faye. They operate Ye Olde Bath Haus, offering rich mineral water that's naturally heated to 108 degrees.

The Gills are the kind of folks who make this town tick. Friendly and accommodating. Neighborly. Nothing pretentious. Maybe it's the water. Clear, clean, hot-flowing spring water. Bubbling up through pebble-lined floors. Hot enough to soak away the aches and pains of a long day's drive.

The town used to be called Hot Springs—an all-too-common name. So in 1950 when Ralph Edwards, the producer of America's most successful radio game show, "Truth or Consequences," asked for a town to voluntarily change its name to that of the show—well, the folks in Hot Springs wasted no time. In a special city election, 1,294 citizens opted for T or C, leaving 295 disgruntled voters unhappy with the town's new moniker.

But today most locals are happy with the city's name—the only town in America to be named after a game show. And don't think Ralph Edwards didn't

Photographs by Mark Nohl

*Above—Sailboating, one of many recreational pursuits that draw visitors to Elephant Butte Lake State Park. **Upper right**—A cultural heritage exhibit at the Gerónimo Springs Museum in Truth or Consequences. **Right**—Thelma Wynne works behind the counter at her combination bar-grocery store-museum in Cuchillo along NM 52.*

appreciate it. Just drop by the Gerónimo Springs Museum on Main Street and take a look at the personal memorabilia Edwards has bestowed upon this marvelous little museum. It also is jam-packed with ancient Indian pottery, turn-of-the-century artifacts and Western paintings. Take a few minutes and chat with the volunteers who staff it; they are experts on the region.

T or C's location astride I-25, New Mexico's major north-south highway, makes it an easy weekend drive from cities to the south such as El Paso and Las Cruces. Travelers from as far north as Denver, Santa Fe and Albuquerque can cruise the interstate into T or C. For those who dislike the monotony of freeway driving, take NM 304 south from Albuquerque and drive through the historic communities of Bosque Farms, Belén, Tomé and Las Nutrias. Rejoin the interstate just above La Joya to Socorro. Then take the side road along the Río Grande from Socorro to San Antonio or farther south through the Bosque del Apache.

NM 185 parallels the interstate north from Las Cruces. You will pass by Radium Springs, Fort Selden State Monument, Leasburg Dam State Park and on through the rich farmlands of Hatch, New Mexico's chile-growing capital. Follow NM 187 to rejoin I-25 near Caballo Lake State Park and in a few minutes you're in T or C.

Retirement and recreation are big business in T or C. The chamber of commerce readily dispenses information about the area. Two golf courses, a municipal swimming pool and a bowling alley add variety to the mineral-bath offerings. The *Herald*, the town newspaper, also produces the *Chaparral Guide*—a free informational handout on the history and events in T or C and Sierra County. Pick up some issues at the chamber office.

T or C's climate compares favorably to Arizona's Sun City and other Western retirement havens. It also offers a military retirement center that's been picked by the Veterans Administration as a model for other states to follow. The New Mexico Veterans Center stands on a hillside overlooking downtown T or C. It is an oasis of shade trees and green grass where visitors are welcome to stop and enjoy a picnic.

Hanging on the center's walls are paintings and other art produced by America's veterans. Some of the works are for sale.

T or C is known as much for Elephant Butte Lake State Park as for its hot springs. The Butte, as some like to call this warm-water lake smack in the middle of the Jornada del Muerto, began in 1912 as one of the first Bureau of Reclamation western irrigation projects. It is now a focal point for summer recreation.

Bass boats, sailboats and speedboats dot this 21-mile-long lake throughout the summer months. Lakeside fishing and camping guarantee a steady stream of visitors. Bass fishing is a popular sport at the Butte. National bass-fishing tournaments are conducted each year, with several scheduled in summer months.

While at the lake, take a drive across the dam's crest. About 1,674 feet long and 306 feet high, the dam holds back enough water to irrigate 155,000 acres of farmland stretching from T or C past El Paso, Texas. Drop by the Elephant Butte Resort for food, drink or lodging or visit the historic Damsite Marina and Lodge built in 1938, a beautiful, tree-lined area where visitors can escape the summer sun. From a park overlooking the old marina, you can watch dozens of sailboats crisscross the lake's deep green waters.

After visiting the Damsite Marina, drive east on NM 51 about 13 miles to the railroad stop at Engle. Cattlemen used the old railroad station, founded in 1879, to ship cattle to market via the Santa Fe Railroad. A few miles from Engle, take a look at T or C's emerging wine industry. A group of investors, planting California seedlings, hopes to produce more than 5,000 bottles of wine a year. Plans call for turning this chaparral-covered countryside into thousands of acres of lush green vineyards.

Take advantage of Truth or Consequences' reasonable motel rates and enjoy several side trips, particularly into the nearby Black Range Mountains, part of the Gila National Forest. An excellent gateway into the Black Range is the old mining town of Hillsboro. Drive south of T or C on I-25 for 15 miles and exit on NM 152. Twenty minutes later you're in Hillsboro, an 1870s boomtown where more than $6 million in gold and silver were mined from the surrounding hillsides.

Today, Hillsboro is like a movie star waiting to be discovered.

The town sits along Percha Creek, which overflows its banks from time to time, sending townsfolk scrambling for high ground. As you enter, the Black Range Museum is on your left, offering a quick and pleasant lesson on Hillsboro's colorful history. As you continue through town, again to your left, high on a hillside, are the remains of the old courthouse, built in the late 1890s, and the town's jail. Rusted iron bars and steel doors are still framed in crumbling red brick. Hillsboro was the county seat for Sierra County until 1938. The county seat was then moved to Hot Springs, now T or C.

If you have time, drop by Hillsboro's old schoolhouse. The schoolhouse, the county's oldest dating back to the 1800s, stands high on a hill overlooking town. When floods came, this is where residents waited for waters to subside.

Today, the schoolhouse is an antique shop and restaurant. If you like, you can buy the plate on which dinner is served. You can roam through the old schoolrooms and inspect hundreds of antiques and assorted memorabilia.

From Hillsboro it's just nine miles farther west to Kingston, another old mining town that once boasted a population of 7,000. Today only a few residents live in Kingston year-round. You can continue on through Kingston to Silver City or return to T or C for the evening.

Another excellent short trip from T or C is to the communities of Cuchillo, Chloride and Winston. With a little backtracking, you also can drive to Placita and Monticello. From T or C go north on I-25 about five miles and take the exit for NM 52. As you head west on this well-maintained two-lane road, you come to a fork where NM 52 splits into NM 142. Stay on NM 52 to Cuchillo and stop at the old mercantile and bar to step back into another era. Cuchillo, Spanish for "knife," was an 1850s stage stop. Winston and Chloride were both mining communities that sprang up overnight when silver was discovered in the area. Only a few residents now live in these once bustling towns, but the visitor still can enjoy the flavor of the Old West.

Turning back toward T or C, take a left on NM 142 for the drive to Placita and Monticello. As you near Placita, you make a quick descent toward the Alamosa River, which cuts through the communities and

empties into Elephant Butte. The two-lane, paved road becomes a well-graded dirt road. Ranching and farming in this isolated area give the visitor a feeling of yesteryear. Old adobe structures still stand, such as the San Lorenzo Church in Placita and San Ignacio Church in the old plaza in Monticello.

Truth or Consequences and the many communities that surround it offer the weekend traveler a fascinating glimpse into New Mexico's history.

Bath Haus operators Faye and Garlon Gill and their granddaughter Billie Faye Tanner.

Right—The picturesque town of Hillsboro, which hosts its annual Apple Festival and Buzzard Days each September. Artists, writers and retirees have moved into the onetime bustling mining community. *Below*—The New Mexico Veterans Center.

Truth or Consequences is the economic and tourism hub for Sierra County. The community is the gateway to Elephant Butte Lake State Park, which draws hundreds of thousands of visitors each year. It also is an ideal starting point for a number of side trips into Sierra County's historic past. Conveniently located along I-25, T or C is an easy drive from major population centers such as Las Cruces, Albuquerque, Santa Fe and El Paso.

POPULATION: T or C, 6,000. Sierra County, 9,500.

ELEVATION: 4,240 feet above sea level.

CLIMATE: The average summer high is 89 degrees, with a nighttime low of 62. In January, the average daytime high is 54 degrees, with lows at night in the upper 20s. Humidity averages 10 to 15 percent.

PRECIPITATION: Average annual rainfall is 7.1 inches.

SPECIAL EVENTS: Each May T or C sponsors the Ralph Edwards Fiesta. In mid-September, the community hosts the Sierra County Fair, with exhibits, a junior livestock show and entertainment. Several major fishing contests also are conducted during the year.

NEARBY ATTRACTIONS: Visit Caballo Lake State Park, several nearby ghost towns and the small communities of Hillsboro, Kingston, Lake Valley, Engle, Cuchillo, Winston, Monticello and Cutter.

OTHER BOOKS PUBLISHED BY *NEW MEXICO MAGAZINE*

New Mexico Magazine
1100 St. Francis Drive
Santa Fe, New Mexico 87503

(505) 827-0220 or 1-800-435-0715